TURNING POINTS

Managing Career Transitions with
Meaning and Purpose

Lisa Severy, PhD
Phoebe Ballard
Jack Ballard

authorHOUSE®

www. turningpoints research . org

AuthorHouse™
1663 Liberty Drive, Suite 200
Bloomington, IN 47403
www.authorhouse.com
Phone: 1-800-839-8640

Printed in the United States of America
Bloomington, Indiana
This book is printed on acid-free paper.
ISBN: 978-1-4343-6548-4 (sc)

Library of Congress Control Number: 2008901206

This book is published in
loving memory of
Jack Ballard
1927–2006

CONTENTS

PREFACE

The world is changing at a faster pace than ever before. New technologies, global communications, diverse populations and shifting expectations drive the changes that impact our daily lives. This rapid rate of change leaves many people feeling uncertain, overwhelmed and confused.

Increasingly, Americans are looking for ways to self-direct and manage their personal life transitions - their *turning points* - including change in careers, finances, health maintenance, family, friends, and community relationships in a balanced and congruent way. Once considered a linear process, planning for the future is quickly becoming a more fluid process and people are looking for various ways to be in charge of their own lives.

Most people have many choices; yet they lack a systematic and conscious approach to make the important kinds of quality of life decisions they face in this world of change. People bounce from one turning point into another without any sense of control. When they take a moment to stop and think about life, many long for a sense of the meaning of it all.

Turning Points offers a systematic approach for identifying your qualities, interests, past experiences, dreams and values that can help you to better understand and even anticipate change. Taking the time to review these aspects of your self will help bring to consciousness what is important. This in turn can lead you to a life plan that will satisfy you and give your life meaning and purpose. Through your own personal discovery, you will be empowered to take charge of and navigate your life transitions. You will develop a mission that provides a context for the many decisions you make as you navigate your turning points.

These strategies are now offered in a "hybrid" workshop format through colleges and various organizations throughout the United States. The hybrid format mixes text books, online exercises and experiential group processes to appeal to a variety of learning styles.

This format has proved to be both fun and effective for mid-career transitioners.

The ideas presented in <u>Turning Points</u> are the culmination of years of practice, research, and theory in the realms of personal and career growth and development. Core concepts include:

• *Free Agency* – No matter who you get your paycheck from, you are the only one that can manage your career. If you've got work today, so much the better, but keep an eye on the news. There are trade associations for just about everything – including the public sector. If you're looking for work, be aware and open to all of your options. While you might prefer the "security" of employment, other avenues exist to find opportunity.

• The *New Impermanence* – The only constant is change. Being successful means successfully managing change. External chaos demands internal self-knowledge and confidence.

• *Transition Management* – The new impermanence invites us to look at the way we approach change. Transition Management is a style of living in which people pay attention to their whole lives and anticipate change: both positive and negative. This is especially important in developing career paths. Rather than focusing on individual choices, transition management encourages people to take a longer view of their life work. Rather than watching every specific step, it encourages all of us to lift our heads and look further ahead. At times we may stumble, but by looking across a broad spectrum we are better able to see an entire picture of long-term success. This in turn makes the short-term change less overwhelming. Imagine having a vision of what you want and how you want your career to move forward. If an unexpected event pushes you into a transition, then having a general sense of direction will make your transition less stressful.

• *Personal Power* - While loyalty and connectedness to organizations do not have to be things of the past, corporate and organizational investment in employees - from hire to retirement - are more the exception than the rule. Professionals must embrace the notion that we are all free-agents working for various client employers throughout our working lives. Accepting this truth helps us to take control over our own transitions.

• *The Gift of the Examined Life* - As with most everything else in life, taking the time to examine and understand our past, present, and future leads to better choices and decisions. Investing time in thorough self-assessment - your accomplishments, successes, values, skills, interests, talents, joys and sorrows—can make the difference between feeling lost and feeling grounded. Self-examination is a gift that we give ourselves and yields tremendous benefits.

• *Deepening Relationships* - Our connection to the world comes through our connection to other people - colleagues at work, family, friends and community. Relationships provide the great treasures of life. Understanding yourself in relation to others is the most important part of being connected to the world.

• *Find Your Passion* – One of the most significant changes in the world of work over the past century has been a shift of expectations. Many people now expect their careers to be personally fulfilling as well financially supportive. New technologies, global communications, and flexible working schedules have brought about a blending of professional and personal lives not seen since before the Industrial Revolution. You should feel empowered to seek a work life that satisfies and an environment in which to connect and utilize your skills, experience, and knowledge with enjoyment and passion.

• *Listening* - When you begin to see yourself as your own personal manager, you begin applying management concepts to your decision-making. Perhaps the most important of those skills is listening. Your own voice – and feedback from significant others - will help guide you through your Turning Points. Good communication depends more on listening well than on speaking well.

• *Vision & Mission* - Like any great story our autobiographies are grounded in themes and values that repeat throughout our lifetimes. By examining and developing those themes as visions and missions we learn to seek opportunities for accomplishing our mission in the world.

• *Invest in Health* – Many of these concepts - the New Longevity, Personal Power, Listening, Vision—all depend upon mental, physical, financial and spiritual health.

• *Go for It!* - As with most everything else, the more you put into your Turning Points, the more you will get out of life!

Managing transitions is a skill like any other. Think of it like learning to drive a car. At first it is difficult, embarrassing, and filled with abrupt starts and stops. With time and practice, it becomes second nature—a process we rarely even think about as we do it. The more you practice and internalize these principles, the more natural they will become.

We hope the ideas, principles, and suggestions within this book will help you turn your life's challenges into opportunities. The concept of work is often burdened by negative energy—burdens, drudgery, fear—and yet replacing that negative energy with positivism can open an entirely new world of personal possibilities in every area of our lives.

INTRODUCTION

May you live all the days of your life.
                                        - Jonathan Swift

In the fast-paced world of the 21st century the only constant is change. Welcome to the age of the "New Impermanence". Call it uncertainty.; call it constant change; call it an unending series of "turning points." As Peter Drucker wrote in 1993, *"Within a few short decades, society rearranges itself. Fifty years later, there is a new world."*

Some people embrace this constant state of flux and uncertainty while others are overwhelmed by it. Turning Points is a model designed to give you tools and suggestions not just for *managing* change, but *exploiting* it in ways that fit your mission and benefit both you and the world around you. Working step by step through Turning Points will help you establish a system for working with inevitable changes so that they work for you. The more you practice and internalize these principles the more natural they will become. As such, this system can be used over and over again. Life is a perpetual learning experience. You'll have plenty of opportunities to practice change management!

Section I of Turning Points explores the new reality of impermanence in our world and the human need to develop new approaches to the future. It will touch on some concepts regarding personal power. The connection between personal power and relationships is essential and makes all the difference when it comes to the achievement of enjoyment, effectiveness and fulfillment.

YOUR PERSONAL CHECKLIST

When the sage admonished us, "know thy self," he or she was right. Each of us has the innate ability to understand our personhood – **Who You Are** as an individual. Section II of Turning Points deals with many different facets of your life. Going over your checklist will help you make concrete what Stedman Graham calls your "ID" – your capabilities, qualities, knowledge and your primary values

– as well as your personal life history – your accomplishments and experiences. These are what make up your story so far.

Who's Special To You? Figuring out who you are often goes hand-in-hand with who the other significant people are in your life. Most of life's important transitions involve others. Making the most of any turning point has a lot to do with coordinating with the special people in your life. Too often our important connections are taken for granted and decisions are made in isolation. Your turning points are a good time to revisit your family, friends, colleagues, community, and memberships. They are vital to your quality of life, yet so easy to take for granted.

In addition to caring, courtesy, and genuineness, communication is the key to maintaining ongoing relationships. The chapter on *Your Special People* is a pitch for intentional receptive listening and understanding as crucial aspects of good communication practices.

How's your health? More and more, people are realizing that responsibility for maintaining their mental, physical, financial, and spiritual health is their own. Medical technology, new knowledge of the benefits of good nutrition and exercise, and an understanding of the importance of reduced stress have combined to add thirty extra years to human life expectancy. It is well worth it to spend a little time and energy to keep your health in mind. If you are in this life for the long haul, you want to be prepared.

Today we know that mental stress can have as negative an impact on our wellbeing as physical stress. Attitude is essential no matter what the challenge: whether dealing with turning points, difficult relationships, or career/financial challenges. Self-knowledge is a key to attitude consciousness. Luckily there are many ways available to you for figuring out and adjusting your attitude, from basic self-help to professional counseling.

How is your spiritual health? It is hard to argue with the vast amount of data indicating that people are happier and more at peace if they are in touch with some sort of a guiding principle for living their lives - an ultimate sense of *meaning and purpose*. Turning Points does not advocate for any form of religion or spirituality, only that it can be helpful to think about and have one. If you know why you are alive and you have a way of contributing and engaging in life that is in alignment with that knowledge, chances are you have good spiritual health.

For many, this is about their faith and belief in a religious or spiritual tradition. For some, spirituality is expressed through practice - what they do every day, such as meditation, prayer, bowing toward Mecca, Tai Chi, or some kind of ritual devotion to a deity. For others, it is more subtle activity such as walking by a creek, climbing a mountain, or going to a Star Trek convention. Your spirituality may be related to your relationship with life itself. By exploring that relationship, you many find the meaning and purpose we all seek.

YOUR WORK LIFE
Do you enjoy your work life? Section III covers several different aspects of how you relate to life at work. <u>Turning Points</u> is based on the premise that work is a natural condition of human life; that work in its essence is service; that work is the basis for a feeling of self-worth; that work is our connection to the world; and that work can be enjoyed and even fun! Workers today have high expectations of the world of work and we think this is perfectly appropriate. We believe that people experience work dissatisfaction because their professional lives are not connected with who they are as people. Just because you are good at something and are professionally successful at it doesn't mean you should be doing it. Encourage yourself to demand more. Demand that your "work life" be tossed out in favor of your "life work."

If you don't think you have enough energy to make that kind of commitment, think about the fate of a frog in a pot of water. A frog tossed into a pot of hot water will immediately leap out. It knows something is wrong and it produces the energy needed to get out. The same frog tossed into a pot of cold water on a hot stove will slowly cook until it dies. It may sense that something is wrong, it may even experience some stress and angst, but there is never enough power to force that frog into action. Please, don't be a frog! Don't simmer in uncomfortable but tolerable conditions until you die (literally or figuratively). Muster up the strength to take a leap of faith.

To help you figure out where to leap into your new life's work, you will be introduced to the *Five E's Formula*. This involves a determination of what you really like to do and really *Enjoy* that is consistent with your personal values. It requires identification of your *Experience* and *Expertise*, as represented by analysis of your accomplishments, qualities, capabilities and knowledge. It also includes *Enquiry* about the constantly evolving needs in the workplace and an attitude of *Entrepreneurship*: a willingness to take risks and manage your own transitions.

Take Charge of Your Career/Life is about career planning as a multi-faceted, ongoing activity. These days employment is becoming more and more individual rather than institutional. You may know people or even find yourself working for multiple employers - even all at the same time! Today there is more flexibility and more opportunity, which can be both a blessing and a curse, depending on your attitude.

Chart Your Lifework Adventure involves actually working to get a picture of your life. There are many ways to use graphic techniques as tools to "paint pictures" of life as we want it to be. This section helps you identify and prioritize what you want: materially, work and family activities, and quality of life. It also discusses what resources you need to achieve what you want: experiences, expertise, knowledge and relationships.

"Preneurship" is the term we use to describe *Personal Branding*. This concept is critical and concerns how you communicate your value, both in writing and in person. It is the external representation of your internal mission. You will know that you have a solid, dependable mission when you can articulate it and explain it in relation to the needs of a given work environment.

HUMAN DEVELOPMENT
The field of human development is relatively young, having only been in existence since the middle of the nineteenth century. Before

that, very little was studied and written about how humans grow and develop. Freud is probably the most well-known (as well as controversial) pioneer in the field. Following his monumental beginning, more recent work has been done regarding a stage theory as a process of maturation. In *Of Human Development* – the findings of Teilhard de Chardin and psychologists Carl Jung, Erik Erikson, Daniel Levinson and Gail Sheehy are discussed. More about the developmental stages and how we learn, change, develop, and mature follows in *The Ages and Stages of Life*.

Every turning point is a potential learning experience. *From Crisis to Opportunity* explores ways of being ready for these major changes that are inevitable. It covers the turning points that are anticipated - formal schooling, work, marriage and children, mid-life issues, and post-career issues as well as the unexpected, unanticipated ones - what Turning Points calls *the devastating D's* - death of a loved one, divorce, downsizing, disease, disability, dependency, depression, and dissatisfaction.

MAKING THE MOST OF TURNING POINTS
While we are glad you are holding a copy of Turning Points in your hands, we have to admit that this isn't enough. The concepts in this book will only work for you if you live and practice them. A journal will help you develop your comfort level with this new look at your self, your life and your career. We recommend getting a notebook and using the *Journal Subjects* at the end of each chapter to guide your writing. You can start by writing down your reasons for acquiring this book and your reactions to the concepts presented so far. A journal is simply a record of your thoughts and feelings - something to concretize your new insights and ideas as they come. Writing them down and expressing them is a great way to enable this book to have a lasting experience.

Another tool to help you make the most of the concepts in Turning Points is the Turning Points Navigator® (TPN) online self-assessment. We have formed the company TPLS Corporation (dba Turning Points) to deliver the concepts in this book to a larger audience. TPN is a hybrid curriculum that employs this book, group processes and online assessments to help people like you to treat your turning point as an opportunity. The TPN online assessments are like a guided journal where you will be asked questions about you and your life. They are really meant for your own use, but of course can be printed and shared with others. TPN is available through Turning Points Authorized Providers. More information is available online at www.TPNavigator.com.

THE GIFTS FROM EXAMINING YOUR LIFE

While change is the new constant, we can learn a great deal from our history. Socrates put this into perspective when he said, "An unexamined life is not worth living". To take the time to stand back, think about, and plan your life is not only helpful, it is imperative. Once you have a clear picture of who you are, what you want, and how you want to accomplish your goals, you can anticipate and use transitions to move you forward. To put it more bluntly, once you get your act together, your life can be so much more interesting, both for you and for others. You can enjoy and appreciate it right up until the day you die.

So many of us are waiting for something better to come along- a better job, a more fulfilling relationship, a nicer house, a more expensive car- how many of us actually put the energy behind making it happen. DON'T WAIT ANY MORE! Examine your life, decide what you want and work towards that mission. You may not always get exactly what you want, but you will know that you have given your all. Often, you will discover something even better along the way. Add transition management and the tools in Turning Points to your inventory of personal assets and *Discover Your Bigger Picture* by giving yourself the gift of the examined life. Take advantage, take charge, take responsibility -- the choice is yours. You will never regret it.

Chapter 1

A New Reality

"Every few hundred years in Western history there occurs a sharp transformation. Within a few short decades, society rearranges itself – its worldview; its basic values; its social and political structure; its arts; its key institutions. Fifty years later, there is a new world."

- Peter Drucker

Many people today feel as if they are caught in a perpetual "spin cycle." They feel as though they cannot keep up with all that is happening "out there," not to mention in their own personal lives. They tell themselves that change is an inevitable part of life, a cardinal rule. Stars explode. Continents shift. Everyone and every thing changes all the time. Nothing lasts forever. Nothing is permanent. *"So what's my trouble? Am I making a mountain out of a molehill?"* they ask.

No, they are not exaggerating. It isn't strange to be feeling that way, in fact, most people do. The new reality is that the world itself is currently going through a turning point – one of the most profound shifts in the history of humankind. A cultural transition is in process right now. As there was a shift from an Agrarian Society to an Industrial Society, today the change is from the Industrial Age to the Information to the Communication Age. These shifts have presented new challenges - and more complexity - than in all previously recorded history. And it isn't over. As we adjust to the 21st century, the magnitude and direction of future changes remains entirely unpredictable. A new world is being created right in front of us.

A WORLD OF CHANGE

We live in a whirlwind of change. True, change has always been a part of life. However, today is said to be different because the severity and rate of change seem to have accelerated. Major change is happening more frequently and rapidly than ever before. We are bombarded by change and face so many choices at the same time that the old rules no longer seem to apply. Because the world has changed so much, what our elders did (or didn't do) no longer serves as a model for our behavior or how we think. It is as if we are not even living in the same world they lived in.

Many things are contributing to this accelerated change. There is, of course, the technology explosion. We have become a global economy; no longer can countries think of their interests alone. Racial diversity is the name of the game all over the world. People are living longer—a change in human experience that has had a ripple effect in terms of retirement, education, health care, family planning, and even elder living arrangements. Not long ago, people took for granted that they would retire around age 65 and live another five or ten years. Now, life expectancy has been extended. We can and should plan to be alive for another twenty-five to thirty healthy years after retirement. These extra years will be a wonderful plus if planned for. To enter a life of total leisure at age sixty is no longer a wise or satisfying choice.

The *New Longevity* is an example of the dramatic challenges that confront us which can have both positive and negative consequences. Many issues need to be weighed carefully such as where to live and work (urban or suburban, anywhere around the U.S. or the world) as well as new life style alternatives which may or may not be desirable or appropriate. Traditional religious life has changed. Many of the old values have dissolved and people are searching for their own sense of meaning. Family life is different for many: people are getting married and having children much later; half the marriages in the United States are ending in divorce; approximately 80 percent of American children are forecast to live in a single parent home for a part of their childhood; the nuclear family still exists but has been joined by the urban tribe; siblings live across the country from each other; aging parents and their families seldom live in the same town.

These are only a few examples of the kinds of forces we are dealing with today. These forces are quickly taking us further and further away from an old picture of life to which many still want to cling and provided stability in times past.

Everyone is struggling to develop a new worldview. This is a new context that fits within a vastly different picture from a hundred years ago, or even twenty-five years ago. Most of us want something that can be identified - a composite reality that would be useful as we adjust to the 21st century. In <u>Megatrends</u>, John Naisbitt says: *"The most reliable way to anticipate the future is by understanding the present."* This chapter includes discussions of five major areas of change in this new world of impermanence. Identifying these powerful forces *en masse*, along with the underlying subsequent pressures they cast will help lessen our stress as we try to think about, plan for, and create our futures.

Change in and of itself is neutral. Change is the ending of one thing and the beginning of something new. Individuals assign meaning to change by thinking of it as good change or bad change. Although we can all probably agree on impact of some change—the death of a loved one is obviously emotionally devastating - the assignment of meaning to change is a very personal process. People often infuse change, especially dramatic change, with some positive and some negative elements. Take a lay-off, for example. The change was unexpected and painful, but ultimately if a person ends up with a better job, it may be viewed in the big picture as a positive change.

Transition, on the other hand, is the way in which we each adjust to change. William Bridges describes transition as *"…the psychological process that the person must go through to unplug from his or her old identity and become reoriented to the new one."* In a sense, transition involves our adjustment to external change - leaving an old job, losing a spouse, having a child, etc. All of this change requires a transition from one reality to a new reality. Most of us think about change from a linear perspective; whether by choice or by circumstance, a movement from point A to point B. Bridges believes that the process of transition is much less straight-forward and is often accompanied by a plethora of emotions. In between the points of A and B is a dip into chaos: fear, anxiety, excitement, depression, enthusiasm, sadness, anticipation, angst, and all types of other emotions. In order to pull ourselves out of that dip, we have to find the energy to climb back up to the top of the loop and take a purposeful step towards the future.

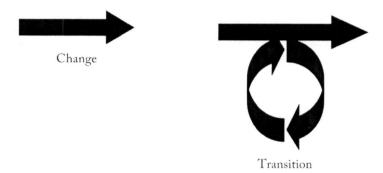

Change

Transition

The amount of change bombarding us on a daily basis necessitates new attention to the process of transition. People who are naturally (or become) adept at transition management adjust to change more quickly and with a sense of purpose. Managing transition is easier when you understand the context of the change occurring.

EXPLODING COMMUNICATIONS TECHNOLOGY
In replacing the Industrial Age, the Information and Communication Age has brought the world the computer, the Internet, and the worldwide web. Direct sales on the Internet involve billions of dollars annually. The technology explosion is most apparent in the fields of medicine and telecommunications, but there is no part of the economy untouched by this dramatic revolution. There is a computer chip in just about everything - from your car to your toaster. Rare is the person in the industrialized world who has never used the internet. Home-based business opportunities have

exploded as computers in every home bring the world of work into the living room while FedEx Kinko's, the UPS Store, and eBay have made office services and product shipping available to anyone. Look at the number of online dating services available and you will see that technology has worked its way into almost every aspect of our lives – and not just work.

There's no stopping this technological explosion, no saying, "hold still until I catch up." We can't predict exactly what new innovations will appear next or how they will impact our lives. We can assume that our work life, home life, finances, health, and family will continue to be deeply impacted. At this rate of technical evolution, it would be impossible to try and anticipate what the future will bring. As one school counselor suggested, helping middle school students to understand specific careers doesn't really help when you have no idea if those careers will even exist when they enter the workforce. Who knows, perhaps our children's most challenging decision will be which planet on which to work!

GREATER LONGEVITY AND A LONGER WORK LIFE

Thanks to the dramatic improvements in medical technology, holistic wellness practices, health information, education, intelligent approaches to living, and affluence, life expectancy in the developed world has increased 25-30 years in the past 100 years. With modern medicine and new insights regarding nutrition, many of us will live well into our eighties - vigorously if we stay involved - and quite a few of us will live into our nineties, even hundreds.

The prospect of a very long life is exciting, and perhaps a bit unnerving. For example, many people in their 90's today are continuing with their interests – if at a somewhat reduced pace. Becoming properly prepared for our longer life span is a must. Being armed with the right attitude and some planning you can go on having fun at work and play for the "bonus years". The new longevity has brought the possibility of working well past the traditional age of 65.

"I am long on ideas, but short on time. I expect to live only about a hundred years".
– Thomas Jefferson

This lengthening of our life spans has been accompanied by numerous changes in our expectations of different age groups. Generally speaking, people are getting married and having children much later than they did even one generation ago. People in their early twenties are still considered older adolescents. In fact, many new college graduates are returning home rather than searching for professional positions or entering directly into graduate school. This gap between college and the world of work is a time of exploration, adjustment, and transition. With the knowledge that we generally spend more of our waking hours at work than we do anywhere else, our expectations of the workplace have also increased. We look for situations that fit with our personal values and missions - work that we actually enjoy.

"And what is it to work with love? It is to charge all things you fashion with the breath of your own spirit."

- Kahlil Gibran

We work long hours and understand that we will be working for many more years than the generations that came before us. Like change itself, our work lives have reflected a movement away from a linear pattern to a more flexible one. Instead of a traditional pattern of education, then work, and then recreation (retirement), many people are creating their own patterns. How many people do you know who have returned to school after working - or even after retirement? How many have taken a sabbatical between jobs? How many are even flexing their schedules to be able to do both school and work at the same time? Let's face it: a typical model no longer exists. We are all making it up as we go.

GLOBAL ECONOMICS AND DIVERSITY

The world economy has become truly global. This means no matter your nationality, you must think globally. Global business means we must be able to accommodate many differences and understand that our way may not be the chosen way for all our business partners. It is not enough that companies and organizations tolerate diversity, but to be successful, they must develop culturally competent workforces that represent the constituencies they serve.

There continue to be challenges in other countries that impact our working lives here at home. All nations of the world continue to suffer from labor exploitation, environmental degradation, military expenditures and tribalism. In the international marketplace, their problems become everyone's problem. For example, US consumers have often punished manufacturers who use sweatshop or child labor abroad. Public outcry has forced them stop. Being part of a complicated worldwide system economically, politically, and socially means that a stone thrown into the lake in one part of the world will cause ripple effects everywhere.

Those who embrace, cherish, and understand the power of diversity will be more successful in the global economy. Remember the Golden Rule of treat others as you would want to be treated? That rule assumes that everyone wants to be treated the way you do. The Golden Rule is now yielding to a more respectful perspective - sometimes referred to as the Platinum Rule: treat others the way *they* want to be treated.

SPIRITUALITY

The impact of powerful, fast, global change has left many of us feeling lost and confused. These feelings have led to a new resurgence in the search for spiritual meaning. For some this has meant more active participation in organized religion. For others, it has expanded into new areas of spiritual growth. It is happening across generational groups. Many Baby Boomers in mid life feel burned out, confused about what it all means, and Generation X'ers feel this burn out and loss of direction in their late twenties when they have graduated from college but are not yet partnered or starting a family.

People are struggling with basic existential questions like 'Who am I?' and "Why am I here?" Spiritual pursuits do not always provide answers, but they do ask important questions:

- What are my ethical values?
- What are my moral values?
- Philosophically, how do I find balance between liberty (individual freedom), equality (of opportunity), and interconnectedness (community and caring)?

- Politically, how can a democracy contain the excesses of a free market economy (capitalism) without stifling creativity by regulation of competition and prices (socialism)?
- In what way do I impact the world and how does the world impact me?
- What is the nature of change and how can I create positive change in myself and in the world?
- Is there a god?

Christians, Jews, Muslims, Buddhists, Hindus, Taoists, Wiccans and Pagans turn to the fundamental rules of their religious beliefs to find answers. The relationship between spirituality and work is a complicated one, exacerbated by the blending of "work self" and "personal self" into one holistic existence. According to a Gallop Poll, 78% of Americans expressed a need for spiritual growth in 1999 compared to just 20% in 1994 and the dramatic and horrifying nature of the September 11th tragedies has made these issues even more poignant.

In examining your life and the way in which you manage transitions, it is important to understand your mission. For some, their mission is closely tied to spirituality while for others spirituality is only a small piece. Thinking about your own spirituality will help you to flesh out your picture and may provide clues to your meaning and purpose.

Summary Points

Secular Christian

- Our reality is a world of constant change and uncertainty.
- The new *reality of change* includes:
    - exploding information and technology
    - greater longevity and a longer work life
    - global economics
    - diversity
    - spirituality

Journal Subjects

- How have you personally been impacted by the five areas of change outlined in this chapter (information & technology age, increased longevity, globalization, diversity, and spirituality)? How would you rate your transition in response to that change?
- Are there particular areas in your life in which you would like to instigate change?
- Are there particular areas in your life in which you are currently anticipating and/or fearing change?
- Are there people in your life who seem to manage transition and change better than others? What makes them different?
- How do you assign value (good or bad) to changes in your life? Does your attitude or basic outlook impact that assessment?

Chapter 2

CREATING NEW PATHWAYS

"We can and should be in charge of our own destinies in a time of change."

-Charles Handy

"Two roads diverged in a wood, and I – I took the road less traveled by, and that made all the difference. "

- Robert Frost

The life journey of our ancestors was usually a shorter, straighter road with fewer turning points. There were fewer choices. Life was simpler. Until relatively recently, most people were born, lived and died in the same area surrounded by multiple generations in the same area if not in the same house. Men often worked at the trade their fathers followed and women worked on the homestead or family farm. Changes were usually in smaller, more predictable increments.

It is the shear number of opportunities and potential directions that make our crossroads so complicated. This is a good problem to have. Think about it this way: How would you like to walk into a bookstore and find only three books? Choosing a story would be much easier, wouldn't it? So why do most of us prefer large bookstores, packed from ceiling to floor with every type of book and adventure possible?

Why aren't we overwhelmed by that choice the way some of us are overwhelmed by the number of potential stories in our futures?

Of course that analogy isn't quite fair. The bookstore is organized to help us find what we need or want. The books are divided into sections, new books are highlighted, and recommendations are made by staff or consumer guides. You can at least partly judge a book by its cover or flip it over and read the back.

The main idea behind Turning Points is that you can treat your life choices the same way you approach your excursions to the bookstore. Figure out what you want, browse the available sections, read the descriptions of your top choices and, most importantly, invest in it. Buy it! Whether that books lasts a lifetime or is finished over the weekend, you can always return for another story.

Personal Turning Points
If we accept the premise that change is the only constant and that death is the only way to stop change, then we can embrace the concept that "to live is to change." It is ironic then that human nature encourages us to resist change every step of the way. The uncertainty of how things will be different causes anxiety and stress. This phenomenon of feeling unstable and in a state of flux permeates every area of our lives. In the world of work, all the rules have changed. Company loyalty, taken for granted even twenty years ago, is seldom experienced today. No one feels the same security in their job as they once did. Because of technological advances, downsizing, and the global aspects of business, we are all like Alice in Wonderland when she said she was running as fast as she could just to stay in place.

All of us must embrace the idea that we are the only ones in control of our working lives. It really doesn't matter whether you are working for someone else or for yourself: you are the Chief Executive Officer (CEO) of your life. Roy's story is a perfect example of how this makes a difference. Roy took charge of his life and his story shows what can happen when someone is smart, understands their values, and manages their transitions in accordance with their mission.

ROY

When World War II began, Roy was just finishing three years of an aeronautical engineering course. Drafted into the army, he applied for officer candidate school and became a maintenance officer on Guam for the rest of the war.

When he returned, he went to work as an engineer in a factory. He could tell almost immediately that this wasn't going to satisfy him. A relative in the textile industry got him interested in that business, and Roy returned to school at night to get applicable training. When finished, he was hired by a textile brokerage business, a near complete switch from his engineering background. He liked it immediately.

By scraping and saving, Roy and his wife put together enough money to buy their own textile company. He grew it, sold it, and bought another – a public one this time. He ended up buying and selling parts of three companies until he had one that is now a national retail chain.

Along the way, one of the original employees – a business-smart young lawyer fresh out of school – became his partner and is now running the business. At that point, with the day-to-day operation in good hands, Roy decided to go and try something else. He joined an industrial company as a consultant for two years, was later made a senior officer and ran the consumer products division.

When Roy became bored with that industry, he left to join a financial services company. When that company was taken over, he and another man formed an investment partnership. Today it is part of a larger firm which includes his lawyer son and his original partner. As a whole, his career covered four completely different businesses - textile, retail, consumer products, and finance.

Roy's story epitomizes the new American success story. Rather than taking an entry-level position and working himself up the corporate ladder, he created new opportunities, augmented his experience with further education, and did not let fear of change keep him in unsatisfactory situations. How did he succeed? He learned by doing; he learned from people with whom he worked and associated.

And he kept going back to school. Whenever he needed to know something, he took a course at night school.

Roy explains the variety of his successful ventures as entrepreneurship. He believes that if you are thinking like an entrepreneur you will meet people and make connections no matter what you are doing. Here is Roy's formula for being a successful entrepreneur in life:

1. Do a lot of listening, watching, and keeping your mouth shut.
2. Be sensitive to people and what they are like. Be a good judge of people. Look for honesty and integrity. Are they perceptive and smart?
3. Maintain high personal standards for yourself. You can't cheat and expect to succeed.
4. Have high personal integrity and a strong moral and spiritual foundation if you want a well-rounded life.
5. For direction, turn to your own intuition and conscience.
6. When in doubt, sleep on it. Your answers will come when you need them.

This way of thinking -Roy's personal pathway- reflects the demands of the new world of work. Roughly one-third of the American workforce is identified as being independent contractors, working for themselves rather than a single employer. Even those of us who work for one particular company or organization should begin to think of ourselves as free agents contracting our skills, talents, values, and contributions to a single employer at a time.

What Is a Turning Point?
Turning points in our lives happen with change - the old no longer exists, and something new is being born. Something happens, and nothing is ever quite the same again. Every turning point, whether purposeful or accidental, can be seen as a new opportunity. They can be planned and wanted changes like getting married, having a baby, quitting your job, moving to a new location or getting that dream job you've always wanted; or unplanned, sudden and unexpected - your spouse wanting a divorce, an unplanned pregnancy, someone close to

you dying, or losing a good job unexpectedly. A turning point can be set off by something as simple as meeting someone new - anything that causes your life as you knew it to suddenly stop and be replaced by something new.

As you have already no doubt experienced, no major change – whether planned or unplanned - is ever easy as in between the time of endings and new beginnings there is always a never-never-land where we feel a bit lost. With none of the old landmarks visible, the skills and patterns we used to organize the old world may not work anymore.

The only predictable things about turning points are their inevitability, and that they all require adjustment. Everyone experiences change - and will continue to until they die. The real question is: how will we view our turning points? Will we view change and transition as an opportunity, or something that happens TO us that can't be controlled or planned? If we don't answer in the affirmative, we end up just drifting and being affected by events rather than the other way around. When change is managed, however, it can mean new possibilities and opportunities. That recognition requires a positive response, which when provided, changes everything.

Turning Points -- The Human Experience

Turning points such as birth, coming of age, graduation, marriage, becoming a parent, the death of one's own parents, and our own old age and death are all part of the human experience. At some level, most of us are emotionally prepared for these changes. We know they are coming. We observe life and have seen that these events happen to everyone. More or less consciously, we think we know what is coming and most of us attempt to prepare for it. We study for our exams in school. We try to date people who are suitable marriage partners. We help our children with schoolwork so they can get into a good college. We buy life insurance. We put aside money to save for the future.

We long for change. Later, when we look back on changes, we see that they were actually major turning points – times when suddenly nothing was ever quite the same. The high school student entered college. The college student graduated and went out into the world to a new career. The newly married couple had their first child. Mothers and fathers of young children dream of the peace and quiet which will return when the last child goes off to college – and then experience the depression of the "empty nest." There are also anticipated changes we dread: serious illness, loss of a loved one, unemployment, divorce.

There are always a few fortunate people who seem to handle changes easily and without any particular planning or conscious effort. On the other hand, most of us tend to respond to events by the seat of our pants, sometimes gracefully, but at other times less so. Many are paralyzed for a time while others just keep going and blunder through – even during positive transitions that were planned and wanted. It is important to remember that it is not just major problems, but sometimes the little things which create turning points and upset our lives.

Turning Points – Opportunities for Growth

There are many turning points which you can anticipate and prepare for. The typical life stage transitions -such as parenting- bring definite obligations. While there are no guarantees in life, chances are very good that your child will grow to maturity and that you will want to provide them with a good education.

Turning points may come about because of subtle shifts in feelings or interests. Sometimes simple discontent can lead to exploration of new ideas. Sometimes a new interest develops gradually over a period of time and eventually leads to a major turning point. We change on the inside as well as outside. Our interests and desires vary with age, experience, and our exposure to new ideas.

The same young man who thinks mostly of girls in his teen years can become the career-obsessed workaholic in his thirties and move on to a spiritual awakening in his fifties. The newly divorced middle-aged woman who feels alone decides to take classes so she will have a broader range of interests. While she may not articulate her reasons for enrolling in the local college, she knows that there is a good chance she will one day want to change her career. She has some interests she has never developed and decides that now is a time to learn more about those interests and try them out.

A turning point can be a time of growth and the catalyst for taking a new path. It is an opportunity to change your attitude, widen your vision for your life (its direction and possibilities), and get in touch with your meaning and purpose.

Every Turning Point Can Move You Forward

A college sophomore has been working toward admittance into a unique and prestigious business program. Unfortunately, his low grades and lack of experience have made admission to the program impossible. He is advised to explore other options but refuses to make any alternate plans and is resentful that he has to. Finally, in a position of choosing a different program or leaving the university, he enrolls in a new program of entrepreneurial studies. He is intricately involved in the development of the program which is highly ranked and very prestigious by the time he graduates.

This story tells of someone who reluctantly found a new path, transitioned from his old view of the future to a new one, and ultimately dedicated himself to new possibilities. That flexibility and his training in entrepreneurialism will be a source of strength to him throughout his career.

Most of us have already encountered many changes in life and must be prepared to handle more. You may have already devised techniques and procedures that have worked for you in the past, or you may have been tossed here and there by change and somehow muddled through. The important thing to remember when any change happens is that there are always many options - always more than one possible road to travel. The way that you decide to manage your transition is as important as the change itself. Turning points imply individual freedom and choice, and at some level we are always in a position to exercise choice – at least about the way we react to events.

Remember the story about the frog in the pot? You *can* do something about your situation. Sometimes it takes a while, but with patience and perseverance you can create a vision for the future and begin making it come true. The rest of this book is designed to help you do that. It will help you to recognize what you want. That is the first step – deciding to take charge of your life and go after what you want. When you know what you want, are in touch with your values and what is important to you, and mix that with the right attitude, you will find yourself empowered beyond your wildest dreams. You can become an expert on yourself through your own individual and independent learning process.

A turning point is a place in the road where it becomes obvious that there are new decisions to be made. Sometimes we create these turning points by taking charge of our lives. Sometimes life creates the turning points and we are only able to take charge of how we react. In either case, the key is **taking charge**. How we react to change is always more important than the change itself. The situation does not control our destinies - our reaction to the situation <u>does</u>.

We are all unique individuals. Reaction to change varies because we have individual temperaments and life experiences. Part of the process of getting to know yourself is becoming more familiar with how you respond to change. If you have never thought about it, you probably don't know. Begin observing yourself and how you react. It may surprise you. No matter what you discover, there are techniques that can enhance the process. If you react by denying that change is a natural part of life, you could be doomed to a lifetime of things happening TO you; of feeling like you are at the mercy of life. This happens at all ages. Think about the college students who fall into a major, graduate, and have no idea what to do next. If they continue to let circumstances direct their existence, they end up moving home or being underemployed in a dead-end position. Most of these students find the strength at some point to push themselves into a turning point - applying to graduate school or seeking an entry-level professional position with potential. From the pain of being lost comes the energy necessary to find oneself.

In her book, <u>A Cherokee Feast</u>, Joyce Sequichie Hifler expresses this point beautifully:

Today may be a turning point. It happens that way - not with flashing lights and fanfare, but quietly...Something in us, something about our awareness, gives us reason to suddenly be conscious of new circumstances and new ideas. We are able to think outside the limits of our usual methods. Life, for no apparent reason, begins to fit together as though we found a piece of the puzzle that completes the picture. As turning points go, some are not particularly great to see, but are often hidden in such small, ordinary events as to go undetected. Our part is to be aware of the change and make the most of it while it is at its strongest.

Riding the Waves of Change

How can you make the most of your situation? Think about surfing the big waves off the coast of Hawaii. The energy and power behind those waves is truly amazing - nothing else like it in the world. Successful surfers know that they have to be out in front of the wave or they can be seriously hurt. They have to anticipate by using all of their senses to read the water, the waves, and what may be coming next. They also watch and listen to those around them. They are not afraid of what's coming because they feel ready. They also practice a lot, which helps them feel confident. The anticipation is exciting, and the feeling of being on top of the wave is like no other.

You can use the same technique. See the waves of change coming, get out in front and ride them in; it is fun and exciting. To ignore either the *new impermanence* or the waves is dangerous. You need to face the fact of the new reality head on. Acknowledge that this new reality is not going to go away. Approach change mindfully from your own unique world view. Make the decision to make the change appropriate and positive for you.

"Even if you're on the right track, you'll get run over if you just sit there."
- Will Rogers

Free Yourself by Examining Your Life

Our capacity to manage change effectively can mean the fullest, most satisfying life imaginable. More than ever, we are on our own. We are free to take responsibility for our lives and become more conscious of our choices; to be discriminating by carefully making decisions; to act on them as we go along; to be in touch with our own desires, talents, values and experience; and to be guided by our deepest selves. One of the primary ways to be prepared for the future is to know yourself.

You Can Take Charge of Your Life

You *can* take charge of your life. Don't get stuck at any future time because you haven't done your homework. Don't just let life happen to you. Live it rather than just letting it live you. Take some time now to evaluate your options. Use future turning points to rev yourself up, not shut down. Remember the analogy of surfing a wave. Do you go with it or fight it? Every day is a chance to start over again. Today really IS the beginning of the rest of your life.

Turning Points is designed to help you get to know yourself well. It will give you "the gift of an examined life" - offering you a life planning system which allows you to get new clarity regarding yourself and the foreseen and unforeseen events you may face ahead. These tools will enable you to deal with the stages of life intelligently as your needs and concerns change - to tailor your life for optimum security and enjoyment. Just like anything else, the more you do it the better you get. Flex these new muscles and become a master at managing your transitions.

You will have a method that you can call on from time to time -as you need it- that is flexible enough to respond to whatever turning point may occur. This method is objective enough to help you arrive at a pragmatic conclusion. Count on the day following the night, and count on many big changes occurring in your future. When they do, Turning Points can give you the tools to move from change into opportunity. It is a noble art worth learning, and one that will make all the difference.

Summary Points

- Living with the *new reality* means more personal turning points.
- Change is difficult for most people.
- A turning point is a change that impacts your life entirely- the ending of the old and beginning of the new.
- Turning points have always been part of the human experience.
- To create new pathways you need to know what you want in life.
- Turning points are opportunities for personal growth.
- Develop an attitude of taking charge of your turning points.
- Don't fear or fight your life changes. Go with them. Exploit them.
- You are free to examine your life, to learn to know yourself.
- Use the following chapters to prepare yourself to handle change positively.

Journal Subjects

- Make a list of at least three life-changing turning points you have moved through in the past. Select one of those and speculate on the results if you had selected a different path.
- Describe a turning point in your life which appeared to be a challenge and turned out to be the best thing that ever happened.
- *"Dream lofty dreams, and as you dream, so shall you become,"* John Ruskin. If money were no longer an obstacle- if you awoke tomorrow with five million dollars in the bank- what would you like to do for the next three months, the next three years, the next thirty years? Create a "blue sky" scenario which includes your most lofty dreams.

Chapter 3

YOUR PERSONAL POWER

"You cannot teach a man any truth. You can only help him discover it within himself."

-Galileo

Generally speaking, our culture teaches us to learn from authority. We come to understand the nature of authority as we grow up - from parents and elder family members to teachers and supervisors. We also learn to trust other authorities in accordance with our own values such as the media, government representatives, religious leaders, or scientists. There is another voice of authority that we tend to downplay in our culture - a voice that has become more and more important as we learn to challenge traditional authorities. To become adept at transition management, we must listen to, understand, and respect our own intuition and inner voice.

You are the most important person in your world. Some may read that statement and believe we are encouraging egotism or self-obsession. Like most everything else of importance, moderation is the key. In a sense, we are advocating self-centeredness; in other words, that the key to personal and professional success is taking responsibility for your own life - your passion, your future - and not deferring your turning points to the control of others. Striking a balance between your needs and the needs of the world around you can be difficult, but you have to accept that you are in control of that balance.

Have you ever been hiking in Yosemite National Park? The overwhelming vastness tends to catch people off guard. You never feel quite as small as when you are looking out into a seeming infinity. There are two ways to respond to that sense of being completely insignificant in the grand scheme of the universe. On the one hand, you can feel hopeless and doubt that you could possibly have an impact on the world. On the other hand, you can accept that the universe is vast, diverse, endless, and does not have the resources to focus on individuals. Each individual must focus on his or herself. The acceptance of that power - power to make decisions, power to choose your attitude and response to events, power to literally change the world - has to come from within. If you are waiting for the universe to do something for you, to owe you something, then you could be waiting for a very long time.

You and your life experiences are your most important and basic resources. Galileo suggests that we begin to search for our truth within ourselves. This is especially important when we are looking for the answers to the larger questions of the meaning of our lives. It also helps to guide us in regard to how to take charge of our search for higher satisfaction and enjoyment or even how to think and behave. Our first reference has to start within ourselves: *What do I think? What does my experience tell me? What are my values in this case?* To be a mature, grounded person, we need to become our own authority. That is what it means to have personal power.

Personal power is a reflection of the people, experiences and environment around us. As we grow, we embrace the things we view as positive and would like to emulate - those things that make us feel most alive - and integrate them into ourselves. At any given moment, we are the accumulation of all that has impacted us since birth. As such, personal power is not only a reflection of who we are at birth, but of our entire life story.

Accepting personal authority - and the responsibility that accompanies it - impacts all aspects of your life. When you accept personal power you take responsibility for your career, your relationships, your happiness, your spirituality - everything. It requires that you stop blaming others like your boss or your parents and start taking action towards new turning points. Take, for example, the story of Margaret.

MARGARET

Margaret was a phenomenal student and flew through her undergraduate degree with little difficulty. She had been planning on a career in medicine as long as she could remember, encouraged by a proud mother and father who accepted nothing less than the best. During her first year of medical school she became depressed, lost weight, and her grades began to slip. Her advisors and parents wondered if the added difficulty and stress was finally catching up with her. She was referred to a school counselor who met with her regularly.

Through a great deal of reflection, Margaret came to admit that she felt disconnected from the goal of becoming a doctor. She had internalized her parents' goals for her without question and sincerely believed it to be her passion too. The further she entered into medicine, however, the less she felt like her true self. With her counselor, she processed her feelings of guilt over disappointing her parents and came to accept that she had to take responsibility for her own happiness and that by internalizing her parents' goals, she had yielded her power. She began exploring other fields and eventually made a decision to focus on research.

When she finally decided to share her experience and her decision with her parents, Margaret was delighted and relieved to know that all her parents had really wanted for her was to be happy, successful, and secure - all things she was finding in her new career.

Personal power and authority are not only important in career decision-making and planning; they have dramatic implications in your personal life as well.

PAMELA AND JIM

Pamela was born when Jim was twenty-three years old. The father and daughter duo were close throughout Pamela's childhood and despite being one of three daughters, they tended to spend the most time together. When Pamela graduated from high school and went off to college their relationship understandably changed. In addition to typical issues of adjustment, Pamela and Jim struggled with some deeper issues. Jim tried to advise Pamela on every issue from classes to roommates. At one point in the semester when Pamela was especially stressed, Jim called one of her professors to ask for an extension. Pamela became increasingly frustrated by his level of involvement and tried to distance herself by cutting their phone conversations short and coming home less frequently. Jim was hurt and frustrated by Pamela's behavior and the rift between them continued to grow.

During a holiday break, Pamela was venting to Ann, one of her sisters, about Jim's behavior. After listening for some time, Ann asked Pamela if she had ever shared her frustration directly with Jim. Ann argued that Pamela was holding Jim responsible for repeating behaviors that he may have no idea bothered her. After all, he was only trying to help! Ann encouraged Pamela to accept her own personal power and share her feelings with Jim. What he would decide to do with that information was his choice; she would be taking control over her response.

As expected, Jim was surprised by Pamela's frustration and made a promise to try and be more respectful of her boundaries. By taking control of and asking for what she needed, Pamela was able to instigate a turning point in her relationship with Jim - a relationship built on each one accepting personal power, responsibility, and authority.

Accepting Personal Power Means Accepting Responsibility

"Look within. Within is the fountain of good, and it will ever bubble up if thou wilt ever dig."
–Marcus Aurelius

Personal power is an *inside* job. You always have choices and options which you can exercise. Accepting responsibility for your life means accepting your personal power to move in the direction of your goals. We all know people who would rather complain than do something about a situation. If you are reading this book, however, chances are good you do not want to be one of those people. In fact, doing nothing about a negative situation - staying in a job you hate or in an oppressive relationship - is making a choice. As Franklin Roosevelt once said, *"there are many ways of moving forward, but only one way of standing still."*

You Have Choices

What does it feel like to accept your personal power? It surely doesn't mean that you can push other people around. Nor does it mean that everything will always go your way. What it does mean is that you feel secure in yourself. You're not swayed by every event or experience. You feel grounded. It means that you can handle rejection and continue to move in the direction of your dreams. A powerful job hunter may not get the first job she applies for, but her sense of self will enable her to continue aiming at the goal and continue searching aggressively.

Personal Power Leads to Inner Peace

When you are in touch with your personal power, you have a general sense that you will be alright - you are on top of your life and you have it under control. You have an inner peace which enables you to deal with whatever comes your way. One of the most popular prayers, used by most of the twelve-step programs for addressing addiction, deals with exactly this issue of personal power. It is the *Serenity Prayer:*

Grant me the serenity to accept the things I cannot change, the courage to change the things I can, and the wisdom to know the difference.

In this context, personal power involves the courage to change the things you have the power to change. Many people never express this courage and therefore, never experience their full power to change the things they can control. They believe that outside events are always out of their control and the best thing they can do is just accept and try to cope. There are several factors which contribute to this viewpoint. One which seems to create the greatest sense of helplessness is the rapid pace of change. Many people feel overwhelmed by the conflicting outside forces pressing in on them. This creates fear and anxiety about the future.

When we rely on outside authority- no matter what the source - we lack the sense of inner power needed to navigate turning points and successfully manage transition. Instead we feel adrift, overwhelmed by the amazing number of options that present themselves, and looking for someone else to tell us what to do. Unfortunately, some traditional career development models feed into this pattern. In an effort to organize and make sense of the vast number of choices, people turn towards standardized vocational assessments that categorize and reduce those options. When used correctly, they can provide useful information about who you are and what you want. When used incorrectly, they can provide a false sense of authority - a sense that this well-regarded career test can tell you what you should be. This is relinquishing your personal power to an outside authority – in this case, a simple set of clarifying questions. It seems silly in this context, but it happens to people in career centers all over the country. It happens because people are desperate to find out who they are, but are not always willing to put in the work necessary to find out. They feel emptiness - a lack of meaning or purpose in their lives- and are looking for a quick fix in order to restore their faith in the future.

How powerful do you feel? You may have never thought of these questions before, so in order to move ahead in taking charge of your life, it is important to evaluate where you are. Here are some simple questions to ask yourself:

- *Do I generally believe what people tell me about myself?*
- *Do I worry about what other people think?*
- *If someone criticizes me, does it bother me for a long time?*
- *Is there someone in my life who seems to be a major obstacle to my happiness or success?*
- *In what areas of my life do I feel particularly powerful?*
- *In what areas of my life do I feel powerless?*
- *If I had more power and control in my life, what would I do differently?*

Few of us feel as powerful as we would like all of the time. We can all increase our sense of power by paying attention to what is going on inside ourselves. If you answered yes to one or more of the first four questions above, you may want to redirect some of the focus of your life journey. You don't want to make a habit of feeling powerless.

Here are some stories of people in all sorts of circumstances. Do these stories sound familiar? These are some stories about "unhappy" people who need to face a turning point.

Years ago, I gave up my career in order to be a full-time Mom. Now my last child has gone off to school and I feel like I'm lost and at a dead end. I can't seem to see what I could do anymore. It all seems formidable because I don't even know what I would like to do. It would have to be part-time. What could I do and who would hire me anyway?

•••••

I am now in my junior year of college and still don't have a clue what to do. Everyone I know has picked a major and knows what they are going to do after college and I'm still waiting for a sign.

•••••

I'm just recently divorced. I had thought I'd be relieved and happier, but I can't seem to get myself together. I find I don't know what to do with my life and now I wonder if maybe I made a mistake.

•••••

After ten reasonably successful years selling computers with different companies, I'm fed up. I've experienced poor management, bad bosses, mergers, failed companies and most recently a lay-off from a downsizing. Now I am unemployed and afraid that maybe I'm unemployable with so many job changes on my resume.

•••••

I am so bored! Every Sunday afternoon I start to get depressed and even a little nauseous at the idea of starting another work week. Why can't I just win the lottery?

•••••

After 35 years in business, I don't know what to do. My company expects me to retire soon and, in some ways, I'd like to. On the other hand, I like working and I can't see myself playing golf and reading all the time. My wife doesn't seem very enthusiastic about the idea of my retiring either. Should I just tough it out? They can't make me retire if I don't want to, can they? In the meantime, all of my best buddies in the company have retired. I'm really feeling lonely and out of it.

• • • • •

Everyone I work with is incompetent. They stand around talking about Survivor all the time and I end up doing all of the work. I can't say anything to my boss because he's one of them!

• • • • •

I'm 47. I have just married for the first time. I love my wife but it is hard going - even after dating and then living together for a few years. She wants to redecorate my apartment which she seemed to like well enough before and she complains when I don't get home on time. I thought that we agreed on most things and now we have arguments the way we never did before. Maybe I'm not the marrying kind!

• • • • •

I have a good job but I'm bored with it and I don't know what to do about it. Should I try to find something else or just go on?

• • • • •

After 20 good years in what I considered a fun industry, my company has just "re-engineered" me out of a job. With a wife and two kids in high school, I don't know what to do. Do I try to stay in management, or should I update my professional qualifications in some way?

• • • • •

I don't mind my job, I'm good at it and it pays well, but I can't help thinking there must be something more. I don't feel like I'm actually doing or accomplishing anything important.

If any of these examples seem familiar, you are probably feeling less than powerful. The truth is that you have plenty of personal power, and you are in a great position to use it. If you are at a turning point in your life and you want to move in the direction of your dreams, you don't have to sit back and let life unfold. You can take charge of your future.

Start by Doing a Personal Power Inventory

Open up your journal right now and start making a list of your accomplishments. It is very difficult to accomplish anything without personal power and this will help you tap into it. Throughout your lifetime, you can remind yourself of your personal power by keeping better track of it - for example, keep a scrapbook or even just a folder of notes, 'thank you' letters and letters of recommendation to read when you are feeling down. Also, make a note of compliments you receive and print emails that make you smile. You can review those on rainy days.

Some people may scoff at these activities and others may believe that it is better to be humble than so sure of yourself. No one is suggesting you go around bragging to other people about what a great person you are. We are suggesting that feeling powerful will ease your life in many ways. Think about the people you most admire - people close to you or famous people that impress you in some way. Most people to whom you are drawn are simply reflecting something you see, or would like to see, in yourself. Although you may not be attracted to arrogance (most of us are not), they probably exhibit a sense of personal self-worth, assurance, and power that you admire.

Being in touch with your personal power is like walking around with your own battery pack. Turning Points is designed to help you evaluate yourself and your situation which will give you a method for breaking through to new pathways for your life. You will have a new understanding of yourself and your world as well as a new perspective on your options and possibilities.

Many people feel powerless to find happiness and success in their personal lives and careers because they don't understand where their power really lies. They waste their time chasing a new love, a new promotion, or a new toy which they believe will make them feel more powerful. But what they really need is to stop looking externally and take responsibility for organizing their own lives. Rather than focusing on outside acknowledgement, they need to look within.

Turning Points will give you new insights about the meaning of your life, see how past experience has led you to where you are today, and how you've grown and developed. All of these insights will connect you to your personal power. Understanding yourself better can make all the difference. As a result, you'll be more useful and productive, confident and in control, more satisfied and together, and healthier in body, mind and spirit. You'll have more trust in the future and your connection to the outside world. If you have a strong center, you'll also be better able to help those you care about.

Summary Points

- You are the most powerful person in your world.
- Accepting your personal power means accepting responsibility.
- You always have choices.
- Realizing your personal power leads to inner peace.
- You will benefit from acknowledging your personal power.

Journal Subjects

- Take a look at your list of accomplishments and select one to write about. Describe exactly how it felt to feel that powerful.
- Select one of the "unhappy" people facing a turning point mentioned earlier and write them a letter of good advice about accepting their personal power.

Chapter 4

WHO YOU ARE

"Before you can decide what you want for your life, you must first understand who you are, what the influences are on your life, why you act and think the way you do. Some describe this as self-awareness. I call it checking your ID. . . You can't understand the world and how you respond to it until you first know yourself. "

- Stedman Graham

Hopefully the first three chapters of this book have given you a firm grasp of the new world of work. In order to figure out how you want to move within that reality, you have to know more about yourself. Traditional career development models focus on one aspect of your life - your personality, interests, or skills - but our belief is that you have to see the entire picture to really make good decisions. In other words, in order to write the next chapter in your life story, we have to go back and read the chapters of your life to this point.

This chapter is designed to help you begin to inventory yourself. Seeing yourself clearly means understanding both your positives and negatives. You need to understand your personal assets – your values, beliefs, qualities, talents, and life experience so far. These are your most important assets in life. They form the base from which you live your life - your naturally given as well as your self-earned attributes that make you the person you are. By figuring out your preferences and the way in which you naturally do things, you'll be able to manage your transitions in ways that feel comfortable. The alternative feels very much like hitting your head against a wall.

YOU WILL NEED YOUR JOURNAL or ONLINE ASSESSMENTS
As with everything else in life, you get out of these activities exactly what you put into them. The more energy, passion, and effort you dedicate now, the more results you will see later. This personal inventory will contain a number of different resources you'll want to refer to later, so now is a good time to pull out that journal or access your online account.

Your Highs and Lows
Have you ever just wanted to stop the world for a while and just check out? That is exactly what you should do before you start this process. Literally, leave your current concerns alone for the time being.

Now, think back in time. Quickly - off the top of your head - name three things in the past that you really enjoyed – a time with your kids, a vacation, a sporting event, a project at work - anything that made you feel true to yourself, most alive, and most successful. Describe those three things briefly in your journal.

Now, think about three things that were really tough – a difficult school subject, a time of illness, a tricky relationship, the death of a loved one, an impossible work assignment- something you wish you could forget. Describe those three things briefly in your journal.

Finally, identify three sources of great pride - significant accomplishments, times when you've been influential, or felt successful. Think about how it felt to be that successful and briefly describe the experience.

Your History - Significant Events in Your Lifetime
You should now have a list of nine memorable events in your life. You may see some as more significant than others, but the fact that they popped into your brain during this exercise means that they have some importance or significance for you. Again, it is important to record the negatives as well as the positives. It is often negative

experiences or events that teach us the most in life. Pay particular attention to your achievements and contributions and remember these "success stories." Consider the things that these events have in common.

Many people approach life management activities by looking at what they think they may need and by attempting to fix things. It is much more effective to begin by focusing on your strengths and your accomplishments as clues to your successful future. Ask yourself these questions about these significant events in your life and record your responses in your journal:

- What are some of my significant events or turning points (like the death of a loved one or a significant illness)? When have I influenced and participated in the change (like graduating from high school)?
- When in my life have I felt most alive? Most like the "me" I want to be? Those moments when I say "YES" to life? What was happening at that moment?
- What are the themes that run throughout my stories? For example: did they all center around my family or my friends? Did they involve helping or leading people? Have they been personal or involved other people?
- Knowing what I know now, how would I have responded to these events differently?

Your Qualities, Values and Capabilities
Digging into the analysis and synthesis of your accomplishments should provide indications of your personal qualities, your personal values, and your capabilities (talents, skills, competencies, expertise) to emerge. Together these qualities represent the essence of who you are at this time in your life. They convey how you function, and what makes you tick.

To take charge of change and manage your turning points requires self-awareness.

Remember that your qualities, values and capabilities are not static. Living requires growth and change. Think of this process as taking a snapshot of who you are right now. It is our hope that through Turning Points you learn this process so that taking these snapshots throughout your lifetime - whenever you are approaching a turning point - will become routine or second nature. Remember when you first learned to drive? You had to think about EVERYTHING and were sometimes overwhelmed by the need to consider so much information at once. Once you've driven for a while those things become so routine you never even have to think of them. Eventually you will get to that level of confidence when it comes to managing your turning points.

Your Personal Qualities
Make a list of the personal qualities that you think apply to you. For example, if your accomplishments included several long-term projects such as raising a family, or research and development of a new product or service, one of your adjectives might be *steadfast* or *tenacious*.

If some of your examples involved physical courage, you might choose the word *brave*. Please don't forget to include both negative and positive traits. If you're always putting things off, include *procrastinating* on your list. Use your accomplishment and experience stories to help guide you. Are there descriptive words you used often in telling your stories?

Hopefully you have created a long, exhaustive list of words that describe you. You should be curious and explore all of these aspects of yourself. In order to take a small, manageable step forward, however, select four or five words on your list that you consider of primary importance. These will be a good place to start.

Your Personal Values

> *"Open your arms to change, but don't let go of your values."*
> - the Dalai Lama

Values are the principles you really believe in - the conscious and unconscious 'rules' that guide your life and the way you live. When you make decisions about change or the way that you are going to respond to it, successful transition must be aligned with your primary values, not someone else's. When a person feels conflicted, it is often due to behavior that does not match that person's values and beliefs. It can be argued that "know thyself" really means "know thy values".

Your values are a unique mix and reflect influences from your parents, peers and friends, as well as your education and life experiences. They are uniquely 'you' and have more impact on your attitudes and behavior than your qualities and capabilities. Stephen Covey states it boldly:

"The key is to align our social values and our personal habits with . . . natural laws that are self-evident and universal. We all inwardly know them. They are common sense. They deal with four areas: our bodies (to live), our hearts (to love), our minds (to learn), and our spirit (to leave a legacy)."

Sometimes people are put in a position of having to choose one value over another. For that reason, it is also helpful to prioritize your values (which ones are essential and which ones would just be nice). Choose three from your list as most important. You now have a checklist of criteria against which to confirm plans that you make at life's turning points.

Your Capabilities
Defining your various talents is often difficult. We are taught to be humble and respectful. Boasting about our skills is not seen as appropriate. Because of that, we tend to underestimate our impact on the world and the level at which we are capable of contributing. Rather than shutting out or narrowing down your capabilities, shout them out. In the immortal words of Mel Brooks, "That's it, baby, if you've got it, FLAUNT IT, FLAUNT IT!"

Looking back at all of the things you've written in your new journal or your online assessments, start to think about all you have to offer.

Ask yourself some basic questions. What can you do? What problems can you solve? What potential problems can you anticipate and prevent? What sorts of 'work' do you enjoy - business, professional, civic, around the house? Are you creative? What types of things do friends, family, and co-workers always bring to you? Think about where your competencies lie, whether in business, government, household activities, community activities, administrative or service activities.

- **Managerial** - interpersonal and administrative supervisory proficiency
- **Technical/Professional** - reflects both academic and on-the-job training
- **Leadership** - personal or position power to make a difference
- **Operational** - track record of productive performance
- **Administration** - utilization of consultative and administrative skills
- **Academic "Knowledge"** - formal schooling
- **Hands-On "Knowledge"** - informal, from the school of 'hard knocks'

Review all your experiences and accomplishments notes. Include expertise you share without cash compensation such as a volunteering, homemaking, traveling, or friendship. Under each of the above categories, list in your notebook every skill or expertise that occurs to you. Certain ones will appear in several categories; do not censor your brainstorming.

Who You Are

> *"The unexamined life is a life not worth living."*
> – Socrates

If you have completed the tasks in your self-inventory you should have a formidable list of your talents, interests, qualities, values and capabilities. Are you surprised? As a collective, are you comfortable with how it represents you? Are there things that are NOT on the list that you wish were there? Would you like to see more knowledge, experience or expertise? Regardless of your self-evaluation, you should be proud of the work you've done to describe your life. Hopefully you're impressed and can see how others will be impressed! If not, what will it take to impress you and others? You have completed the first steps in being able to make the absolute most of your life and what it can lead to in the future. The adventure has only just begun.

In her book <u>Return to Love</u>, author Marianne Williamson wrote:

Our greatest fear is not that we are inadequate. Our deepest fear is that we are powerful beyond measure. It is our light, not our darkness, that most frightens us. We ask ourselves, who am I to be brilliant, gorgeous, talented and fabulous? Actually, who are you not to be? You are a child of God. Your playing small doesn't serve the world. There is nothing enlightened about shrinking so that other people won't feel insecure around you. We were born to manifest the glory of God that is within us. It's not in some of us, it's in everyone, and as we let our own light shine we consciously give other people permission to do the same. As we are liberated from our own fear, our presence automatically liberates others. Walk gently, breathe peacefully, laugh hysterically!

For most people, it's hard to let the light shine - too many are unsure just exactly who they are. Bringing your many attributes and accomplishments into focus has hopefully given you some light about who you are. This kind of an exercise can take you a step further towards making a difference in this world. You have something particular and special to give.

Up to this point we have asked you to exclusively focus on yourself. That is where the process begins. Now we will ask you to expand your focus to the significant others around you. John Andrew Holmes expressed this point well when he said, "*It is well to remember that the entire universe, with one trifling exception, is composed of others.*"

Summary Points

- Your experiences have helped to shape who you are. The way you remember them and their significance give you important information about who you are and what is important to you - your life themes. These are the internal pieces that other people may or may not be able to see.
- Your accomplishments help you tap into the measurable, quantitative data of the past. These are the external pieces that other people can see.
- In managing change, stay true to your social and personal values.
- The more connected you feel to what you are doing, the more passionate you can be about it.
- Your attitudes and behavior reflect your qualities, values and capabilities.
- Your values are the principles you really believe in.
- Apply your qualities and capabilities in alignment with your values.
- Know who you are, take charge, and set your goals with confidence.

Journal Subjects

- What are your obstacles to taking charge? Candidly, take a look at your limitations or weaknesses. Note any people you could talk to or actions you could take that would help you overcome such barriers to managing your turning points and reaching your goals.
- Examine one of your negative experiences or unsatisfactory job outcomes and discuss what sort of positive learning resulted.
- Focus on two or three particularly enjoyable and gratifying accomplishments and note the personal qualities and capabilities common to them (or uncommon to them).

- What are your strongest points? Are there certain combinations of qualities and capabilities that optimally support your realization of your most important values? Identify what you might do to enhance both your family and your career priorities.

Chapter 5

SIGNIFICANT OTHERS

"Seek first to understand, then to be understood...communication is the most important skill in life...empathic listening... means listening with intent to understand... getting inside another person's frame of reference...we should remember that effective interdependence can only be built on a foundation of true independence...the most important ingredient we put into any relationship is not what we say, or what we do, but what we are."

-Stephen Covey

A crucial aspect of who you are concerns your relationships - past, present and future. Just as you may not have given much thought lately to your experiences and accomplishments -or to your personal qualities, values and capabilities- you may not have taken enough time to reflect upon your relationships and how they impact your response to change. It is too easy to take relationships for granted- especially when those relationships are doing well. By taking the time to think about how we interact with others, we can take another important step towards self-management. Healthy relationships need energy for commitment, time for communications and respect for differences. It helps to clarify your priorities among family, friends, colleagues, and community.

Covey's admonitions are demanding. Empathic (or receptive) listening while being your authentic self can be difficult. At times we hide our authenticity on the assumption that others may not like or respond well to what we have to say. How often have you held your tongue or suppressed a thought in an effort to maintain harmony or keep the peace?

On the flipside, how many times have you gotten into trouble by expressing yourself when others could not or would not appreciate your comments? Combined with good communications skills, recognizing your special relationships completes the self-awareness work needed to be conscious of who and what you are – all of which you need in order to take charge of your life's turning points.

Your Family
Family is a concept that means something different to everyone. It is not important how we define family, only how you do. Generally speaking, people think about family as those related by blood or by marriage, but that narrow definition is changing over time. Today's gangs, religious groups, communes and "urban tribes" are all examples of new definitions of the concept of family.

Those who have a loving, supportive family are the lucky ones. Members of these families know each other inside and out - and love each other anyway. Our families provide our first sense of connectedness to others and tend to help us in establishing our basic attitudes and ideas about relationships. Those who are privileged to grow up in a caring, nurturing, accepting atmosphere in turn find it easier to pass that spirit of sharing into their future relationships. They grow into adulthood expecting to give and receive love, thus setting the scene for others with whom they are in relationship to do the same thing.

This is of course an ideal, and most 'normal' families do not neatly fit into that category. In fact, according to one expert, 97% of all families are dysfunctional to some degree. There are presumably as many different ways to miss the mark as there are families, and all of us probably wish our families had been able to bestow more of that magic elixir which would have prepared us for assured success in life.

Our assumption is that both the 'hits' and 'misses' in a family are all part of the package as it is supposed to be. Our families provide us with our most important opportunities for growth and enable us to develop, discover and move on. In a very real way, our families are our laboratories for learning how to live in the world.

Maintaining good relationships with family members has never been easy. As we've discussed throughout this book, constant change may be the root of these frustrations. People grow, relationships change, our needs become different, and our patterns of interactions change. If one family member changes at a different rate than another, it can be difficult to find common ground. One sibling might compare him or herself to another. For example, with parents and children, the child needs to be able to go from the total dependency of infancy and childhood to the growing independency of adolescence to the eventual interdependency of adulthood. This is necessary for maturity. Later on this pattern begins to shift to the other direction as the parents begin to reach old age and depend more on their children. Each change along the way demands adjustment, attention, and sensitivity if strong relationships are to survive.

Today, there are more conditions that make this even more difficult and complicated:

- Families in our country are often spread from coast-to-coast, making daily interactions more difficult. The nature of our family communication changes from face-to-face interactions to email and phone calls. While these forms of communication are not better or worse, they are different. Family connections take more of an effort to maintain.
- In our world of constant multi-tasking, people are forced into prioritizing everything, including relationships. Extended family, especially those living farther away, tend to be less involved in our daily lives.

- An important part of growing up is differentiating ourselves from others - first, the family, and then from the crowd. To see ourselves as individuals and to live according to our own values in the fullest sense of the word is a continuing task of reaching maturity. This means pulling away psychologically from the family at the same time as hanging in there with them – not an easy balancing act.

Most people believe that staying close to family is worth the effort demanded by modern society. Not only does the "give and take" of relationships make life rich and fulfilling, it also provides a connection to your roots and family history.

Hopefully, your family plays a nurturing and supportive role in your life. If they do, treasure that. If your family doesn't quite fit into that ideal description, it is important to remember that you have control over your response to your family. First, you can pick and choose your attitudes about relationships, and you do not have to be absolutely true to the behaviors you learned at your parents' knees. We all of have to adapt our ideas to suit the world we live in. Even those who come from the most loving of families must grow up to handle today's complex society. Second, you can find significant "familial" relationships outside of your blood relatives and create a family support system of your own that better suits your needs.

Your Parents
Your parents were probably your first connection to the world and many of your interpersonal patterns were established during that time. Whether you are conscious of it or not, many of the ways you respond to others has to do with what was modeled for you in early childhood. As we become adults, many of us make a conscious effort to either emulate our parents or try to avoid some of the pitfalls we have seen them fall into. Have you ever heard something come out of your mouth that sounds exactly like something your mom or dad would say? Regardless of whether you want to be just like your parents, completely different, or somewhere in between, you use that initial relationship as a frame of reference for most others. Those of

us who have lost parents or never knew them often seek clues to who our parents were in an effort to know ourselves.

In addition to maturity differences that make us interact with our parents differently at different times in our lives, there are also generational differences that impact our relationships. The generation entering the workforce in 2005 has been labeled "Generation Y" or the "Millennials". Of the many things that separate this generation from the ones before is that they seem to be much more connected to their parents. This is evident on college campuses, wherein parents participate in every aspect of their child's education. At a meeting of the National Association of Colleges and Employers (NACE) in 2004, one of the session speakers asked the employers in the room to stand up. She then asked those recruiters to sit down if they had ever been contacted by a parent. Every person in the room sat down immediately. Most everyone was thoroughly surprised by the idea that parents would be contacting employers regarding their children, but the presenters were simply illustrating a generational difference that all of us will need to understand.

Romantic Relationships and Marriage

Strong relationships are based on mutual respect and good communication. Because hope is stronger than a wish, below are some hopes for you and your romantic relationships:

- That your partner is your best friend and helpmate and you feel good about your relationship.
- That your partnership provides you strength and energy rather than regularly draining it.
- That you have open communications -on the touchy subjects as well as the easy ones.
- That you're in touch with what brought you together at the start.
- That the two of you get away as a couple from time to time.
- That you and your partner share your dreams of the future and you think *big* about your future together.
- That if you're unhappy about something and there is no resolution in sight, you will seek help from a

professional and get it. There is plenty of help available for just about any issue, and if you have reached an impasse about some issue, the time to resolve it is now. The longer a disagreement festers, the harder it becomes to solve, so don't wait.

- That you make your partner your top priority in your life and that you take the time to make him or her feel special.

Anyone who has ever been in a long-term, committed relationship will agree that it isn't easy. At the same time, most who have been able to weather all the adjustments necessary to make it through agree it is worth it. There is the old story about the man who had a bracelet engraved for his wife on their forty-fifth anniversary that read: *Thank you for forty-four wonderful years.* When questioned if he had counted wrong, he explained that the missed year took into account all those days that weren't so wonderful! One out of forty-five is pretty good!

Your Children

Most people who have children would agree that it is both the most difficult and the most rewarding work you can do. You work terribly long and hard to bring them up. At times the struggle may seem impossible. Parenting can be sheer drudgery. It demands patience, endurance, self-sacrifice, effort, strength, and courage. At the same time, children are a lifelong delightful addition to the meaning of your life and worth all the hard work.

Like everything else in our world, parenting has changed significantly over the last generation. Both parents are expected to participate in child-rearing. With most couples dependent on two incomes, the need for external child care is a fact of life for most families. In addition, the increased divorce rate has created more single-parent and blended families- new sources for relationship confusion and delight.

Wise parents understand that these marvelous creatures we call our children are only on loan to us. Our job is to offer them protection, love, and nurturing for only a very short period. This creature must be sheltered and given sufficient freedom to develop into the person it is meant to be. Then, when the time comes, this beloved he or she must be allowed the freedom to go their own way. The wonderful news is that if the job is done well, parents are often invited to go along and enjoy the rest of the ride. Our job well done, our greatest of joys comes from our children.

Being Single

Romantic partnerships are not always available or desirable for everyone. Whether by choice or by circumstance, being single today has lots of advantages. In fact, many people previously married report they like being single more than being attached. Historically, there was a stigma to being single, but not so much anymore. Attitudes about living alone have changed dramatically in recent years and single persons are now recognized as a significant group. Being single does not mean being disconnected and those who are happy and successful at it have usually created their own system of support. The significant turning points of becoming single or forming a partnership are transitions that can be managed effectively or can become a significant source of stress.

Your Friendships

Friendships are one of life's greatest gifts. Friendship is the perfect follow-on to the subject of being single and free. One of the things we are free to do is have lots of different friends to do things with. The poem, *A Friendship Like Ours*, by James Kavanaugh captures our thoughts beautifully on this topic:

A friendship like ours is without pretense or barriers
Where no word is without consequence, no pain without compassion,
When time means nothing and distance is as insignificant as astral travel
Where a single word can sometimes say all there is to say,
And love grows organically each passing day,
Where misunderstandings are impossible and words have no currency,
Where a chance meeting is enough to last a lifetime,
And heart speaks to heart in a single contact.
I have known good and gentle men and women for a lifetime,
Have been bound to them by blood and debt and every circumstance,
Even lashed together by work and space and passionate concern,

Yet few of these could invade the privacy of my inner being
No matter their power or brilliance, beauty or wealth,
But you were destined to reside there, my friend by an eternal edict,
Because even before we met, you were already there!

Good friends are one of the great gifts in life. A turning point is an excellent time to think about your friends. There are certain stages in your life when friendships may seem difficult to maintain because your attention is demanded elsewhere. While you may wish to be more social and genuinely want to be with your friends, you may not have much time to cultivate your friendships. A lunch once in a while, a Christmas card with a note, or just a phone call shows your friends you care.

You may also find that your selection of friends is based at least partly on convenience. Those with whom you spend the most time may become your best friends; co-workers, neighbors, members of committees, people who enjoy playing sports with you or even people you meet on the net.

Your Community
One of the ironies of modern life is that the increase in the technology of communication has actually made us less connected to each other. Sure, you can email a friend across the world or call your mom between classes so you wouldn't have to be alone with your thoughts while you walk across campus. But you work so much that you don't really know the neighbors next door except to wave at the mailbox. Some fear that these changes have led to disconnected communities.

Community participation is an important way in which we feel connected to others no matter which aspect of it we choose involve ourselves in – the neighborhood store, the local post office, the doctor's office, the homeowner's association or a faith-based club or organization. All of these ties help us create the sense of belonging. Dr. Ralph Ahlberg told a story about Charles Plumb, a jet fighter pilot in Vietnam that illustrates this need for connectedness with humanity. What we are – our integrity, loyalty and dedication to our others - is what is important in the long run.

CHARLES PLUMB

After 75 combat missions, Charles Plumb's plane was destroyed by a surface-to-air missile. Plumb ejected and parachuted into enemy hands – beginning six years imprisonment which he survived.

One day, later in his life, he and his wife were sitting in a restaurant in a strange town when a man at another table came up and said, "Plumb! You flew jet fighters in Vietnam from the aircraft carrier Kitty Hawk!"

"How in the world would you know that?" asked Plumb.

"I packed your parachute," the man replied. The man pumped his hand and said, "I guess it worked."

Plumb assured him. "It sure did. If your chute hadn't worked, I wouldn't be here today."

That night Plumb laid awake thinking about the man. He said to himself, "I wonder what he might have looked like in a Navy uniform. I wonder how many times I might have seen him and not even said, "Good morning, how are you?" or anything else because, you see, I was a fighter pilot and he was just a sailor."

Plumb thought of the many hours the sailor had spent on a long wooden table in the bowels of the ship, carefully weaving the shrouds and folding the silks of each parachute, holding in his hands each time the fate of someone he didn't know.

It is important not to ignore our needs for community. In the busy modern life we lead, it is easy to forget the fact that there is a community out there if we look for it. To deal with this problem there is a movement in many big cities toward neighborhood or block associations. Often these associations offer the same sense of community that flourishes in small towns. If you have moved to a large city from a smaller community and feel lonely, you may find your answer in such an association. If there isn't one, think about approaching some of your neighbors and starting one. Neighborhoods in big cities can be like small towns. Writer and director, Nora Ephron, says she thinks of her neighborhood on the

West Side of Manhattan as a small town and tried to convey that feeling in the film.

Being in a community means being "present" for each other in a way that makes us feel acknowledged and responded to. It reveals itself as a smile, a look, or a handshake. Community is characterized by cooperation and mutual support. The way people respond to us helps us define who we are. Our self-image develops and grows through our relationship to the community around us. More than we realize, we are shaped by our communities. A strong and solid community around us becomes even more important today when our extended family isn't nearby. We need caring people around us.

Bill Moyers once said, "*Civilization … is a web of cooperation joining people to family, friends, communities and country, creating in each of us a sense of reliance on the whole, a recognition of the self in companionship with others, sharing a powerful loyalty to the common good.*" Live and let live isn't enough. It has to be more - live and help live.

Community is not dead in today's America. Though not talked about enough, expressions of community spirit do exist in many places. A recent death proved to us that the community spirit is alive and well when a young father of three young children died very suddenly at his home in a small suburban development in Colorado. Dozens of families - many that the family hardly knew - did everything they could to console the family. They organized and brought in every meal, took in and fed the out-of-town relatives who came for the memorial service, thought through every detail of the service to which several hundred came, helped to clean up afterwards; and then continued to lend support by helping with the children and chores. With such generosity and strength of community, the weight of the tragedy was lessened.

This introduction leads us to two simple questions. WHO IS PACKING YOUR PARACHUTE and WHO'S PARACHUTE ARE YOU PACKING?

In order to get a complete picture of who you are, you will also need to sketch out some information about who you are in relation to others.

This will impact every part of your life and your turning points. For example, were you frustrated in your last job because of the work itself or because of an annoying boss or co-worker? How did your poor working environment impact your romantic relationship when you couldn't get home before 8:00 pm every night? Relationships have a huge impact on your daily life.

Role Models and Heroes

People have been discussing the merits of role models and mentoring for years now. What we often forget to think about are the underlying connections that help us to feel drawn to that person or feel admiration for them. Think about a person that you admire a great deal. This can be someone you know personally or someone famous. Think or write in your journal about his or her accomplishments. Describe what you particularly admire about this person. What qualities do you admire? Why? What qualities would you like to emulate?

Although it is an amazing gift to have a mentor or role model in your life, finding that "perfect" person is not always easy. We can also examine our relationship to others through characters and composites. For example, think about your favorite fictional character. This can be someone from a book, movie, play- anyone you'd like. As you did with your role model, think about the characteristics that person exhibits that you would either like to have for yourself or find in the people around you.

Communications

We usually tend to think of communicating as speaking, but listening is actually a much more important part of communication. The person who is a good listener is always welcome. Good listening does not mean just keeping quiet and letting the other person talk. It means hearing not only the words the other person is saying, but "mirroring" the *feelings* expressed through those words.

Turning Points calls this ability to listen well and really hear what the speaker is saying "receptive listening." Covey calls it empathic listening; describing it as attempting to understand the other person's frame of reference. When you listen in that manner, you are showing respect for other people and what they have to offer. Allowing them to express themselves freely, without interruption, enables them to feel their own individuality and to grow. This kind of listening is so valuable and rare that people pay big prices to psychiatrists and therapists for it.

In Dr. Rachel Naomi Remen's book, *Kitchen Table Wisdom,* she describes the gift of a good listener:

I suspect that the most basic and powerful way to connect to another person is to listen. Just listen. Perhaps the most important thing we ever give each other is our attention. Just take them in. Listen to what they're saying. Care about it. Most times caring about it is even more important than understanding. Most of us don't value ourselves or our love enough to know this. It has taken me a long time to believe in the power of simply saying, "I'm so sorry" when someone is in pain. And meaning it.

One of my patients told me that when she tried to tell her story, people interrupted to tell her that they once had something just like that happen to them. Subtly her pain became a story about them. Eventually she stopped talking to most people. It was just too lonely. We connect through listening.

When we interrupt what someone is saying to let them know that we understand, we move the focus of attention to ourselves. When we listen, they know we care. A loving silence often has far more power to heal and to connect than the most well intentioned words.

It's not too much of an exaggeration to say that being able to communicate well is the most important skill in life. As you get older, good communication is a gift you can give to the people around you - your partner, children, grandchildren, friends and associates. How many times have you heard someone remember a loving grandparent who really listened to them and made them feel important? Listening to people very carefully makes them feel esteemed, understood, even blessed.

Maintaining positive connections with your family, your friends and your teammates at work depends on your commitment and your willingness to be a good communicator. Ann Lander's list below of

Ten Commandments For Getting Along With People has some pretty good clues about participating well in relationships with others:

1. *Keep the brakes on your tongue; always say less than you think. Cultivate a low persuasive voice. How you say it often counts more than what you say.*
2. *Make promises sparingly, and keep them faithfully, no matter what it costs.*
3. *Never let an opportunity pass to say a kind and encouraging word to or about somebody. Praise good work, regardless of who did it. If criticism is needed, criticize helpfully, never spitefully.*
4. *Be interested in others, their pursuits, their work, their homes and families. Make merry with those who rejoice; with those who weep, mourn. Let everyone you meet, however humble, feel that you regard him as a person of importance.*
5. *Be cheerful. Don't burden or depress those around you by dwelling on your minor aches and pains and small disappointments. Remember everyone is carrying some kind of load.*
6. *Keep an open mind. Discuss but don't argue. It is a mark of a superior mind to be able to disagree without being disagreeable.*
7. *Let your virtues, if you have any, speak for themselves. Refuse to talk of another's vices. Discourage gossip. It is a waste of valuable time and can be extremely destructive.*
8. *Be careful of another's feelings. Wit and humor at the other person's expense are rarely worth it and may hurt when least expected.*
9. *Pay no attention to ill-natured remarks about you. Remember, the person who carried the message may not be the most accurate reporter in the world. Simply live so that nobody will believe them. Disordered nerves and bad digestion are a common cause of back-biting.*
10. *Forget about yourself, and let others "remember." Success is much sweeter that way.*

Networking

As this chapter has focused on people, communications, and interpersonal relationships, it is important to emphasize the role people will play in all of your turning points. This is especially important in your career and vocational choices. Experts tell us that most jobs and promotions are not listed in public- not in newspapers, online, or in trade journals. It may be cliché to say, "It isn't what you know, it's who you know," but that doesn't make it any less true.

There are numerous ways to get your network established and working for you. Here is a list of things that may be helpful for you:

- Make a list of people you know well, their career fields, and their place of employment. You will be surprised by the extent of your list. This is the network you already have.
- Explore professional development opportunities in your community. These could be formal groups like professional associations, chambers of commerce, or informal writing groups or book clubs. These activities will help you add to your network.
- Let everyone in your network know that you are at a turning point and would like assistance. You've heard of the concept of *Six Degrees of Separation,* that all of us are connected in some way within six steps? Networks can function in the same way. For example, you may not personally know an attorney, but someone in your network probably does. By letting your network know that you would like to meet with an attorney, you'll find more referrals more quickly that you thought possible.
- Use your network when you reach out. People will be more likely to take your call and/or meet with you if they understand your connection. When you call or email someone new, tell them how you found them.
- Practice your introductory skills. Meeting new people is second nature for some people and can be painfully difficult for others. If you are extremely

introverted, you may find this networking process very difficult. As with everything else, we recommend small, manageable steps. For example, when you first sit down on an airplane, don't dive straight into your book or magazine. Introduce yourself to the person next to you, ask them where they are going and what they do. Most people enjoy talking about themselves when given the opportunity. Set a goal for yourself of taking the effort to meet one new person a week. In a year, your network will have expanded by over fifty people!

Informational Interviews

One of the best ways to find out about a new situation is to simply ask people "in the know." We come to most turning points with a wide range of ideas and assumptions, some of which are right and many of which are dead wrong. How will you know the difference? Asking pointed questions of people who have experience with that particular turning point will help you navigate more easily without making all of the same mistakes. Your network can be helpful in pointing you towards people to interview. Here are some pointers to help you get started:

- According to Howard Figler, there are five potential goals of informational interviewing: background research on a field of work, researching a particular type of organization, finding out where the jobs are, exploring a particular organization, and speaking with someone with the power to hire you.
- Remember that this is not a job interview (although sometimes jobs do emerge from the interaction). When you call a contact to ask for an interview, introduce yourself, state the purpose of the interview, request a meeting (including the anticipated length), and be clear that you are looking for information, not a job interview.

- Like any other type of interview, prepare ahead by developing a list of goals for the interview and questions that will help you get there.
- Make sure to arrive for the interview on time, dress appropriately, stick to the time limit you originally proposed, and take notes.
- Follow up each interview with a personalized 'thank you' card.

As Stephen Covey put it, "*Seek first to understand then to be understood.*" To be understood is to be accepted. This is what everyone wants - what love and relationship is all about. To be loved is to be appreciated and accepted for who one is. We cannot change anyone else, just as no one else can change us. We can only accept them as they are. We can only change our own behavior and our own minds and attitudes.

In addition to considering how others influence our turning points, it is important to use our network of family, friends, and colleagues to actually help us make changes.

Summary Points

- Your special people are key to who you are.
- Good communications are essential to strong relationships.
- *Receptive listening* enhances communication.
- Your family members are significant people by definition; the first people to shape you.
- Your partner continues that role by helping you navigate your turning points.
- While you only borrow your children from the universe, their connection to you can last a lifetime.
- The single lifestyle is more common and more accepted than ever before; it has its own rewards and frustrations.
- Those with whom we interact- friends, colleagues, community members- are our connection to the world.
- Understanding and expanding our networks can be helpful in coping with various turning points.
- Informational interviewing provides an important tool for expanding your network.

Journal Subjects

- Create a family tree. Next to each person on your tree, add some notes to describe your relationship with that person, a few words you would use to describe that person, and their career field.
- Describe a recent occasion when you felt you were really listened to. Why was the event significant? What was the importance of feeling heard at that moment?
- Discuss your friendships and relationships at work. How have those relationships impacted your job satisfaction? How would you like it to be different?
- How would you characterize your network? Can you think of a time when you met someone through happenstance and ended up becoming friends or colleagues with that person?

Chapter 6

YOUR PHYSICAL HEALTH

"What about the positive emotions? If negative emotions produce
negative chemical changes in the body wouldn't the positive emotions
produce positive chemical changes? Is it possible that love, hope, faith,
laughter, confidence, and the will to live have therapeutic value?"

– Norman Cousins

Healthy Longevity

Since the turn of the nineteenth century, thirty healthy years have been added to life expectancy. Life is very different than it was before the advent of organ transplants, antibiotics, open-heart surgery and the polio vaccine. Fortunately, we are now better prepared to take responsibility for our personal health than any previous age in the history of humankind. Twentieth century medical discoveries have created amazing differences in the longevity and quality of our lives.

Baby Boomers have been the driving force in a movement toward a more comprehensive approach to healthcare. They have moved the context from sickness to wellness. In the process, taking responsibility for one's own health has become a high priority. Furthermore, the Boomers have been willing to experiment with alternate methods and have found many of them helpful, bringing new ideas to mainstream medicine. It is estimated that about 75% of the population uses one or more alternative medical treatments, some to complement or supplement mainstream medicine, others to replace it.

The Body/Mind/Spirit Connection

It is now widely understood that good health involves the physical, the mental and the spiritual parts of us and that none of these components can be ignored. Medical doctors routinely include mental health questions in the process of diagnosis of physical illness.

Since the 1960's, the subject and practice of holistic health has come of age. Practices that seemed kooky then are accepted today. For example, acupuncture is now widely used in the Western world. Heart disease and cancer have been linked to stress and negative emotions. Homeopathic, Chiropractic, Osteopathic and Naturopathic medicine are accepted and practiced. Activities associated with body, mind and spirit are each viewed as part of the whole.

Stress

Stress in and of itself is not good or bad. For example, starting a new job is stressful, but it can also be exciting and rewarding. Having children may be the most stressful thing a person can do, but it can be the most rewarding as well. It is not stress itself that causes someone to be unhealthy; it is handling, dealing with, or coping with stress well that is the killer. Life without some stress would be dull and uninteresting indeed. However, being stressed out most of the time is a different story. If that is your situation, step back and take a look at yourself and your life. Is there a way to simplify? Are you trying to do too much? Is something bothering you that you just can't get your finger on?

Coping with stress is a skill that can be learned. Like any other skill, some people seem to do it naturally and others need much more practice. Here are some characteristics of people who handle stress well:

1   They acknowledge their concerns and worries about the future and prioritize them in order of urgency and importance.

2 They allow all the things on their mind to surface. They do not stuff their worries or challenges away in some dark recess, wishing they'd go away.

3 They do not harbor anger or resentment. Those negative emotions are   poison.

4 They learn to deal with those things they can change and set aside the things they cannot.

5 If they get stuck and feel unable to process things alone, they seek out help from significant others, family, friends, or professional help.

Growth vs. Aging

"If I had known I was going to live this long, I'd have taken better care of myself."

- Eubie Blake

The good news here is that you will probably live a long time. You also know that the kind of health you will enjoy as you continue on through your life is largely up to you. You can take charge of your life now and make changes that will influence your health in later years.

The subject of aging has received a lot of attention lately, and yet there is still much misinformation. Aging is sometimes feared and has even been thought of as a disease. There was a time when becoming fifty was considered a step toward the grave. Advances in medicine, increased life expectancy, and fewer misconceptions about age have given us a new viewpoint. Fifty just doesn't look the same now as it did in 1900 or even 1950. It is indeed a new day in the arena of health and healing.

Not everyone can have perfect health until they die, but today the chances are greater than they've ever been that our healthy years will be prolonged. The key to making your future years turn out to be healthy and full of happiness, whether you are twenty, thirty or fifty, is having the right attitude and good health habits. If you haven't got those in order, start now, no matter how old you are.

You have access to information and techniques to extend your life, and most important, take control of your health. Good health is largely going to be, as it was in the past, a natural outcome of some pretty simple habits in your physical behavior, and a reflection of your beliefs and attitudes.

Because we live in a society which idolizes youth, many of us worry more about looking young than staying physically youthful. Don't confuse your vanity with your ability to function well. Rather than being annoyed by the minor inconveniences of growing older, adopt a positive attitude. Aging is a privilege. As Satchel Paige asked us, "how old would you be if you didn't know how old you was?"

Making Healthy Choices
The holistic approach to health issues provides everyone with the opportunity for self-responsibility, for healthcare, and for taking charge of one's own aging process. What a wonderful gift! There are three distinct parts to physical health care; medical problems (generally treated with drug therapy), surgical, and preventative self-care. It is in the realms of self-care and self-responsibility where some of the most exciting and important developments have taken place.

Because body, spirit and mind are no longer seen as separate, the holistic view of the person as a totality of humanity has risen to a well-deserved and widespread acceptance in healthcare. Experts estimate that sixty to ninety percent of visits to primary care physicians are for issues caused by or exacerbated by stress. While there are many ways of treating the symptoms associated with these problems, addressing the underlying issues is important for long-term health.

We do not advocate the rejection of conventional medicine, but rather the supplementing and complementing of those practices with self-care, prevention and nutrition. In our culture of fast food and fast fixes, we don't do a very good job of managing our lives in ways that increase the probability of long-term health. Good diet, good exercise, and attention to your stress level can help you be prepared for expected or unexpected turning points. It is your choice, your body, and your life. You can approach your health choices with the same "preneurial" attitude that you handle your career and your finances.

The habits which promote good health can be developed. They will contribute to the quality of life - and probably add longevity.

Regular Exercise

Many Americans work in positions that require little to no physical activity. This problem is exacerbated by additional time that we put into our careers. The fact of the matter is that energy feeds on itself. If you feel tired and lethargic and decide to "take it easy", then you require more and more down time. On the other hand, the more you exercise, the more energy you will have - and the more active you will be.

Good Nutrition

Good nutrition means putting the best fuel into your body and avoiding those which are not. Our culture is fascinated with messages of "quick fixes" and fad diets that promise a greater sense of well-being. On the other hand, common sense tells us that the key to good health is balance. Your positive choices will have an immense effect on the quality of your life in the long run.

Smoking

While there has been a dramatic reduction in the number of people who smoke in this country, there are still many people who choose to smoke. If you are a smoker, you may be reading this and thinking "smoking is my choice, which is none of your business." We agree completely. Arguments about second-hand smoke aside, the entire premise of this book is that everyone should manage their own lives to the best of their abilities. We ask you only to consider the notion that your health will be directly impacted by your decision to smoke. If you do decide to quit, there are numerous people and programs available to help you - don't feel like you need to go it alone.

Understand Your Health Insurance

The sheer number of options in our current health care system can be overwhelming. Turning points, especially those which are career-related, are often accompanied by a change in health insurance. Before you accept a new position, make sure that you understand all of the associated benefits, including health insurance. Some health care companies focus on treatment while others focus on prevention. If you have a choice of companies, plans, and programs, be sure to thoroughly research and check each one. If you are going independent or have decided to become an entrepreneur, there many health insurance options available for you as well.

Summary Points

- All the parts of ourselves – body, minds and spirit – are connected.
- Stress is natural and you can learn to deal with it in a healthy way.
- While aging is inevitable, *how* you age is within your control.
- Now is the time to take charge of your physical health by developing healthy habits of food choice, exercise and stress reduction.

Journal Subjects

- Write about one older person you have known who enjoyed life and lived well. What did this person do which you would choose to imitate?
- Take a look at your current life and list the ways you handle stress.
- What would you like to add to or subtract from the mix?
- Name one small, manageable step you could take to lead a healthier life style.

Chapter 7

YOUR MENTAL HEALTH

"The sad things that happened long ago will always remain part of who we are, just as the glad things will, too. Instead of being a burden of guilt, recrimination and regret that constantly makes us stumble, even the saddest things can become a source of wisdom and strength for the journey that still lies ahead."

-Frederick Bueckner

Everything you think, every emotional feeling and every interaction you are involved in has an impact on your overall health and therefore, happiness. Mind, body and spirit are intimately connected via a complex, miraculous network of nerves and cells that make up your endocrine, immune and nervous systems.

Mental Health = Health

The fact of the matter is that your mental health can have a dramatic impact on your overall health. Health care professionals will readily tell you that patients with a positive attitude are more likely to recover - heal more quickly - if they have a positive attitude and a good support system. On the other hand, stress, anxiety, and depression can all have negative impact on your health. Your choices have led you to the place in the road where you now are. Your choices were based on your personal values and beliefs at the time. In a sense, this belief system creates your universe. It causes your successes and it can also cause your disorders. The reality is that what you *think* impacts how you *feel*. Furthermore, how you feel has a direct impact on your results, success, and happiness in life.

We develop an inner storage bank of attitudes, habits and patterns to deal with current life situations as they occur. Some of those attitudes and habits will be helpful to you throughout your life and serve you well. Some, on the other hand, were useful at one time, but may be no longer helpful to you now. Your reaction to turning points in your life will greatly depend on your attitudes and beliefs. When facing turning points, it is important to take a look and re-evaluate what to keep and what's holding you back that could well be discarded. In what areas are you stuck? Could you make some changes now? Consider breaking up some patterns and finding new ways to do things.

BARBARA

Barbara had always put her family first. In the first years of her marriage, she stayed at home with the children while her husband rose to great heights in his career. She was suspicious that he was unfaithful to her from time to time, especially when he was away on long business trips. She never confronted his behavior because she wanted to preserve her marriage and protect her children. She had always believed that holding a marriage together was the most important thing a woman could do.

When her last child went off to college, Barbara realized she was at a major turning point in her life. She found a good counselor and joined a women's support group. Within six months, she discarded the idea that her marriage must be preserved at any cost. She decided to get up her courage and confront her husband with the fact that she was hurting and their marriage was in serious trouble. To her surprise and relief, she found that he did care and agreed to try to open up their relationship again. Though not always smooth, they worked their way through their problems and found new joy in each other. Along with their marriage, she also renewed herself. Their marriage took on a whole new life and they lived happily ever after.

Challenge as a Turning Point

You can get stuck in many ways. Mental attitudes and beliefs that prevent you from enjoying complete fullness in life need to be reexamined. Don't let old ideas inhibit your freedom. Don't let old messages received from parents, teachers, siblings or the environment you grew up in rigidly control your approach to life. "That's the way I think," or "That's the way I am" can be very self destructive attitudes.

The opportunity to grow and change depends on your ability to re-examine, select and discard ideas, habits and patterns. Above all, don't let your life be guided by some preconceived idea of appropriate behavior based on age. Twenty is not too young to begin saving. Thirty is not too late to switch careers. Forty is not too late to begin a family. Fifty is not too late to go to school. Sixty is not too old to start a business. Seventy is not too old to fall in love. Eighty is not too old to work.

Living Your Values

People tend to develop symptoms of mental health problems when there is conflict between their values and their behavior. For example, they may genuinely value peace and harmony and find that they are often quarreling with their spouse. If they refuse to quarrel, they feel downtrodden; if they do quarrel, they feel as though they are "wrong." Conflict creates unhappiness and may actually affect our health. It is not the quarreling that causes unhappiness, but the belief that quarreling is bad. Some "happy" families quarrel a lot. They believe that being outspoken "clears the air" and keeps the lines of communication open. Other families may never quarrel and be just as happy. They use more subtle forms of communication and feel perfectly understood. Problems arise when one person does all the quarreling and the others keep quiet and resent their own silence.

Conflicts with others are often a result of conflicting values. Just as often these differences in values can perpetuate the conflict. One partner's infidelity is ignored because the other partner's belief system dictates that confrontation and separation must be avoided at all costs. One person continues to work for a demanding and unreasonable boss because of a fear of being laid-off.

Conflicts between values and behaviors can also be internal. This often happens when we feel depressed or otherwise unhappy at work. You do your job and you do it well, but you don't really feel any connection to it or to the people around you. Perhaps one of your values is *being appreciated* and no one in your office seems to value you, or your value is *to help others* and your current work situation offers no element of service. In these cases, a turning point requires change in one of two ways; changing the value or changing the behavior. You may decide that *being appreciated* or *helping others* is something you can live without. Alternatively, you could start looking for a transition to a situation that better matches those values.

When our belief system constricts our freedom to choose, the results are often manifested as poor physical or mental health. Mental health problems may be labeled depression, anxiety, neurosis or any number of other conditions. However you label it, new beliefs must replace the old to resolve the internal conflict.

Depression

Turning inward to do some self-examination may be sufficient to get you back to a better frame of mind, but help from outside is often needed. According to the National Institute for Mental Health (NIMH), depression is the 4th "most devastating" illness. About 15% of all women suffer from depression in their lives but less than a third seek any form of help.

Depression can be the result of an internal conflict in values, a difficult situation such as the loss of a loved one, or a general sense of unhappiness. As many people face turning points in their lives, they may experience a certain amount of confusion or depression until they get through their turning point. Anyone who has been "down" for several weeks needs to take care and pay attention. If you find yourself unable to find enjoyment in anything, perhaps even taking to your bed (or wanting to be there) and not wanting to get up, you may be clinically depressed. Seek help. Go to your physician and talk to him or her about your problems. Your physician may want to send you for a consultation with a therapist or psychiatrist, or may prescribe any one of several new drugs to help battle depression.

There is no shame in asking for help when you need it. Consulting with a professional and/or using medication appropriately can help you get to a place where you can start to address your problems and navigate your future.

The symptoms of clinical depression include:

1. trouble sleeping
2. diminished interest in everything
3. feeling guilty
4. low energy
5. poor concentration
6. poor appetite
7. psychomotor agitation or retardation
8. suicidal ideas

People suffering from depression don't usually have ALL of these symptoms, so when any four of them occur, a person should be encouraged to seek help. Depression can be caused by any number of things, including a physical problem. No matter what the root cause, anyone with unresolved emotional issues such as old hurts, anger, fears or feelings of guilt can experience depression.

In his autobiography, *Memories, Dreams and Reflections*, Carl Jung described his own experience with major depression. He recognized and held to his conviction that depression offered a source of potential meaning and value for people who are willing to try and learn from it. According to Jung, this is the point of many myths and fairy tales, as well as poetry. In fact, these types of feelings - that life is precarious and that we are alone and isolated – are normal. Most psychologists agree that most people suffer from this kind of psychological condition to some degree at some point in their lives. It goes with the process of maturation. It was Jung's conclusion that our quest towards wholeness requires us to reconnect to those things we hold as our foundational "core values". Jung believed that this process of reconnection with our most important values and beliefs is an essential task of living.

Counseling and Therapy

When someone is in the grasp of depression, it can be very difficult to find peace alone. As we've said all along, it takes energy and passion to anticipate turning points, and depression is often accompanied by the exact opposite. Counseling or therapy can be very helpful in sorting out these issues. Turning to a trained professional can give someone just the spark they need to improve by encouraging self-knowledge and personal growth. In the past - and even at times today – counseling and therapy have been stigmatized by stereotypes and misinformation; such as the belief that only "crazy" people would need that type of help from a mental health professional. Luckily, today we live in a time when most people understand the benefits of seeking help when needed to cope with the common, "normal" issues of every day life.

One of the great aspects of counseling is the permission to be completely selfish and to focus totally on you. Even if you have a friend that is a good listener, you have to offer some reciprocal assistance. In counseling it is all about you. There are no words to adequately describe what it is like to be able to be completely free with another person without judgment. We can take as much time as we need. We can sit, stand, pace, yell, cry, pound the floor, dance or weep for joy. Whatever and however we are at the moment is accepted, respected, and valued.

Getting therapy means finding someone who is well-trained and experienced to listen to you. Be a good consumer and find someone who fits your needs. If you meet with someone and you don't feel comfortable, find someone that you can be comfortable with. It is important to have a counselor or therapist you trust. If you are suffering from stress, depression or other mental problems that are interfering with your enjoyment of life, we urge you to do something about it. Get good professional help. You can find someone in private practice, a public agency, someone covered by your health program or even a staff member in your company's Employee Assistance Program. A good therapeutic experience is simply an opportunity to talk about yourself and your personal issues with someone who gives you full attention and will keep your confidentiality. Think of this person as a sounding board whose purpose is to give you the freedom to talk yourself out. You will probably discover parts of yourself that you never knew existed such as negative messages that may be holding you back or untapped power needing to be free. You will discover that you are your own best healer. The road to your own healing and wholeness is within you.

Spiritual Counseling & Forgiveness
Rabbis, priests and ministers can also help you sort out your values, behavior and emotions and renew your mental health. If you feel particularly connected to a spiritual advisor, ask that person about counseling. In many spiritual belief systems, the concept of forgiveness is central to the healing process. By discussing issues with a trusted advisor you may find forgiveness for past hurts, mistakes and disappointments. Usually that means forgiveness of others as well as our own faults and limitations. Forgiveness doesn't mean forgetting, which usually means denying or repressing our problems or pretending they never happened. Forgiving ourselves or someone else means finding a way to integrate the pain and accompanying messages and moving forward. Through forgiveness, it is possible to see how learning and growth have come from our turning points. Forgiveness means saying "yes" to healing the old wounds, allowing you to remember them *differently* and live beyond them. In his book *Telling Secrets*, Frederick Bueckner described the psychological and spiritual catharsis that can take place in a good therapeutic experience:

We cannot undo our old mistakes or their consequences any more than we can erase old wounds we have both suffered and inflicted. But through the power that memory gives us to think, feel, and imagine our way back through time, we can at long last finally finish with the past -- in the sense of removing its power to hurt us and other people and to stunt our growth as human beings. . . . Memory makes it possible for us both to bless the past, even those parts of it that we always felt cursed by, and also to be blessed by it . . . I think {this} is what forgiveness of sins is all about -- the interplay of God's forgiveness of us and our forgiveness of God --and of each other.

A couple of words of caution: Objectivity and confidentiality are critical in a therapeutic relationship. While talking with your friends is great, don't try to use a friend for "kitchen therapy." Choose a trained professional who is recommended by someone in whom you have confidence. There are many good mental health professionals to choose from, including counselors, psychologists, psychiatrists, and clinical social workers. Be sure to do your homework and make sure your trusted adviser is trained and certified. Also, be cautious about consulting a spiritual advisor you do not know well. Be sure that not only is he or she trained in the "art of listening", but also that his or her belief system and values are in alignment with yours.

Support Groups

One of the most beneficial phenomena of the last fifty years is the rise of support groups designed to help people help themselves with specific mental health issues. These groups offer a special form of peer counseling which help people deal with their situations and/or heal the symptoms. There are groups for single parents, gays and lesbians, people with any number of health challenges, men, women, all sorts of specific issues and turning points in people's lives.

Alcoholics Anonymous is a great example of a thriving support group. Over two million people have managed to stop drinking and return to normal lives through this brilliantly successful program. AA's "Twelve Steps" are now the foundation of many other groups that deal with other issues such as co-dependency, drug addiction and compulsive sexual behavior. If your mental health issues appear to be intertwined with alcohol or drug use, we strongly suggest you begin your search for stability by attending a *Twelve Step Program*. It may be the very help you need.

You Deserve Mental Health

Mental health will remain a priority throughout our lives. If something happens to upset your emotional balance, the intelligent thing to do is to seek help and never give up until you are back on track. Some people try to accept and live with their problems rather than trying to improve. Don't be someone who is caught in a cycle of negativity. You deserve to be happy and healthy, and life is short. You can learn to live an emotionally healthy, well-balanced life despite any experience. Through openness to emotional health, we can all take steps to create and maintain a healthy mental state. As in every other segment of your life, a take charge attitude makes all the difference.

Summary Points

- Mental health is an important part of your total health.
- Obstacles can be positive turning points if we decide to learn from them.
- Values versus behavior conflicts can cause mental problems.
- Depression is a common concern for most people at some time in their lives. It can be seen as a new opportunity for growth.
- Therapy is a recognized way to cope with the difficult times and can be very beneficial.
- Spiritual counseling also offers a practical way of helping yourself gain mental health through forgiveness.
- Support groups help sustain and solidify new insights and behavior.
- Accept the idea of mental health as normal - and your birthright.

Journal Subjects

- Describe the first major crisis or turning point in your life and how you weathered it.
- Are there any beliefs or ideas you currently hold which stand in the way of perfect mental health? Are your ready to change those ideas? If so, write them out, cross them out, and replace them with a new idea or belief. For example "I am too old to change" is crossed out and replaced with, "I am just the right age to change some more."
- Based on this chapter, ask yourself whether there are symptoms of depression in your life currently. If so, create a written plan to deal with those symptoms.

Chapter 8

YOUR SPIRITUAL HEALTH

"The world is our school for spiritual discovery."
- Paul Brunton

*"During the past thirty years, people from all the civilized countries of
the earth have consulted me. I have treated many hundreds of patients...
Among all my patients in the second half of life - that is to say, over
thirty-five - there has not been one whose problem in the last resort was
not that of finding a religious outlook on life."*
-Carl Jung

People find meaning and purpose in various places. Through both
nature and nurture, we establish a set of beliefs about ourselves,
the world, and the greater meaning of it all. Philosophers, authors,
poets, and spiritual advisors have been thinking and writing about
the meaning of life since the beginning of human existence. For
thousands of years, people have used religion and spirituality as a
vehicle to discover meaning. In the new reality of American culture,
religion is a topic that inspires a variety of conflicting emotions
– oftentimes within the same person. While many continue to
embrace the tenets of organized religion, others search for personal,
mystical links to spirituality and meaning.

Why do we bring this up here? Why is Spirituality important in the context of turning points? Quite simply, there is a spiritual dimension to any turning point, whether you choose to label it that way or not. In a sense, this relates to topics addressed in previous chapters, such as personal power, values, beliefs, and meaning. By spending some time thinking about your own spirituality, you may discover more information to help you in managing your transitions.

In his time, Jung suggested that the clergy and psychotherapists join forces. In a sense, this has come to pass in modern forms of religion and psychotherapy. Both areas have embraced a greater emphasis on the core values of spirituality, the power of positive thinking, and the importance of living an "integrated" life.

Religion

Institutional religion has had a volatile history during the twentieth century. In the emergence of the scientific method, scientists spent a good deal of time and energy trying to disprove the concept of God. The pendulum has now swung back and the concept of 'Intelligent Design' has emerged as a blending of religious belief and science that is troubling to many scientist and "religious" people alike. As Albert Einstein reminded us, "Science without religion is lame; religion without science is blind."

For most of us, the concept of God as an all-knowing, all-powerful old man with a white beard is no longer credible. Literal interpretations of biblical writings have become suspect, and that has driven many away from organized religion in search of more personal meaning. Many young people in the West have left institutions such as Judeo-Christian churches, synagogues and temples and are exploring Eastern traditions such as Buddhism, Hinduism and Taoism, or other nature-based "alternatives", such as Wicca, Paganism, or Native American spirituality.

Spirituality

In a 2005 Gallup Poll, 80% of participants indicated that they are convinced God exists. At the same time, 83% indicated that religion has a very important or important role in their daily lives (compared to 86% in 1985 and 92% in 1965). Interestingly, when participants were asked if the importance in religion was increasing or decreasing in the United States, the response was surprisingly even with 50% responding *increasing* and 46% *decreasing*. According to the Gallop Poll, religious service attendance has been remarkably stable over the years with 44% reporting attendance within the past seven days in 2005 and 41% in 1939.

Herbert Benson, professor at Harvard Medical School and author of *The Relaxation Response* and *Timeless Healing* has made a strong case for the idea that human beings are just naturally "wired for God" (Jung would certainly agree with him). Benson points out that as long as there have been humans, we have worshipped. He contends that faith is rooted in us genetically - encoded in our very makeup. We instinctively know that our faith and our worship are good for us.

Forty-one percent of Americans attend church, synagogue, or temple weekly- remarkably the same as it was fifty years ago. Older people who never left the church behind are joined by younger people who are returning to search for ways to deal with the complexity of modern life with all its challenges. More cautious and less confident than their parents at the same age, they are aware of a need for the moral values and integrity they see missing in society. They seem drawn to religious practice and are finding that religion gives them a strong base for all aspects of life.

In the sixties, many Baby Boomers began looking elsewhere for their answers and discovered major religions other than Christianity and Judaism. They discovered a universal core, but found differences in the role of spirituality. Many Eastern languages have no direct translation for the word "religion." As God is an integral part of everyday life the distinction between "religious" and "secular" does not exist. As the forms and context are different, so the messages carry similar themes and myths. Some people go to Japan and India to sit at the feet of Buddhist monks or Hindu yogis trying to find their answers. While this type of quest attracted a certain amount of ridicule 20 years ago, it is now common to find Americans who attend Eastern religious services or follow a spiritual leader from the East.

Many traditional churches have responded by developing a stronger sense of spirituality – in contrast to religious dogma. In a sense, the spiritual renaissance we see now is non-denominational. Not only are the Eastern religious practitioners numerous and widespread, but people who attend traditional churches are picking and choosing their places of worship based on the spiritual experiences which are offered rather than intellectual belief or doctrine. People care much less about denominations and have no compunction about church-hopping because of certain aspects they are looking for - such as a good Sunday school or preacher, or an educational program they wish to attend.

The quest for new expressions and symbols has resulted in a vital search for a new spirituality and ways of getting around the earlier inhibiting beliefs. This search for spirituality has recently been reinforced by medical evidence that church goers tend to live longer, healthier lives. Prayer and meditation have also been linked to increased healing. According to the Association of American Medical Colleges, 73% of medical schools, including Harvard, offer courses in non-traditional healing methods which include meditation and prayer. Meditation is commonly used to treat chronic pain, high stress, blood pressure, heart disease, depression, cancer and high-risk pregnancies.

Part of the excitement associated with our culture's return to religion is the acceptance by many that self responsibility extends into the spiritual realm. There are a number of newly recognized tools available, some of which we'll explore here. Incorporating these tools into your life will help you to access them during your turning points.

Meditation & Prayer

Eastern traditions, Jewish and Christian mystics, and monks have long understood the personal power that comes from prayer and meditation. The challenge is to transfer the inspiration that results from experiences of silence and quiet time into the loud and sometimes rough world – the world of change, chaos, stress, and even violence and terror.

Albert Schweitzer addressed this directly when discussing his outlook on life:

To the question whether I am a pessimist or an optimist. I answer that my knowledge is pessimistic, but my willing and hoping are optimistic. Two perceptions cast their shadows over my existence. One consists in my realization that the world is inexplicably mysterious and full of suffering; the other in the fact that I have been born into a period of spiritual decadence in mankind. I have become familiar with, and ready to deal with each, through the thinking, which has led me to the ethical and affirmative position of Reverence for Life. In that principle my life has found a firm footing and a clear path to follow.

Our daily lives are bombarded by messages of all kinds. Communication through email, cell phones, advertising and pundits of all persuasions constantly barrage us with more information. With all of this external stimulation, are we losing our ability to just *be* with ourselves? Do you pick up your cell phone every time you find yourself alone for five minutes? Do you turn on the television or radio the moment you get home? We have become so accustomed to the noise and so adept at filtering out, that we may be losing our ability to really listen to our internal voices and the messages that come to us from intuition.

Meditation and prayer can help bring us back to a state of personal grounding. They give us the silence and the space necessary for self-discovery. Making "quiet time" a part of your daily routine is especially helpful in times of transition.

Thomas Merton described it in this way:

If you descend into the depths of your own spirit... and arrive somewhere near the center of what you are, you are confronted with the inescapable truth that, at the very root of your existence, you are in constant and immediate and inescapable contact with infinite power.

Meditation is a great way to calm your brain, gain clarity, and see things in a different light. Meditation has become a source of powerful personal self-understanding to legions of people. Meditation practices do not necessarily connect with any religious practice. Atheists and agnostics meditate too. As Deepak Chopra observed: *"Meditation is not a way of making your mind quiet. It's a way of entering into the quiet that's already there — buried under the 50,000 thoughts the average person thinks every day."*

Your beliefs are an important aspect of who you are, although they may be mostly unconscious. They could be outmoded, destructive messages that play and replay in your head and run your life in ways that you aren't aware of. Meditation provides a means of first becoming aware of those repetitious messages and then turning them off and replacing them with new ones. Not only may you get healthier thought patterns that offer an entirely different outlook on life, but you may also gain practical ideas for proceeding.

There are lots of ways to meditate. Like anything else, it is important to find a mode and method that fits and feels comfortable to you. Therefore, you will probably need to do some research to find your own method. We offer the following steps as a basis for getting started. It is a compilation of some common aspects of different methods:

1. *Find a comfortable chair and sit with nothing crossed, feet flat on the floor, hands resting on your thighs. You may want to keep something to write on next to you in case you have an insight you want to record.*
2. *Close your eyes to enhance your concentration.*
3. *Relax your body one step at a time. Start by flexing and the relaxing your hands, then your arms, then your shoulders, and on through the rest of your body. Simply tense and release to let the tension slowly seep from your muscles. Try to visualize a sense of comfort pouring over your head and down your body all the way over your feet and onto the floor.*
4. *Pick a healthy focus word or phrase firmly rooted in your belief system; a word that has importance and significance to you.*
5. *Breathe slowly and naturally, and, as you do, repeat your focus word, phrase or prayer silently to yourself as you exhale.*

6. *Assume a passive attitude. Don't worry about how well you're doing and don't be mad at yourself if you become distracted. This process takes practice. When distractions come to mind, simply take note of them and gently return to the repetition.*
7. *When insights come to mind, process them and write them down.*
8. *Close your eyes and gently return to the breathing and repetition.*
9. *Continue for ten to twenty minutes. When you first begin meditating it is helpful to try to do it daily. When you become more comfortable, you'll find your own rhythm and know how often you need it – from many times daily to once a week.*
10. *When you are done meditating, open your eyes, but don't stand up immediately. You want things to come back to you gradually rather than being bombarded.*

Prayer & Personal Power

The difference between prayer and meditation is that, in general, prayer assumes a higher power or an external force to which you are addressing yourself. The practice of prayer provides another resource available to you for examining your life and can help you find solutions to your problems and concerns. There are countless different perceptions and approaches to prayer. Use whatever technique or approach that works for you. Don't worry about whether or not you're doing it right. Like meditation, creating a regular schedule for when, where, and how you pray can help you to develop a routine. Kahlil Gibran reminds us, "*You pray in your distress and in your need; would that you might pray also in the fullness of your joy and in your days of abundance.*"

Journaling

Writing in your journal can be as effective as prayer or meditation in connecting with yourself and your spirituality. Whether insight comes as a result of your writing, or you are simply recording those insights, the act of writing it down brings it further into your conscious reality. Meditation, prayer, and writing are tools for helping you take charge of your life and reclaim your personal power. They are efficient, simple and flexible. You can actually do them anywhere. Apart from all the other benefits accruing from the practice of meditation and/or prayer, the setting aside of private and alone time in the midst of busy schedules is worth its weight in gold. If you don't do it already, try it! There's nothing like it to begin or end your day.

Dream Work

Dreams are messages from our "core" that emerge when we are able to turn our conscious minds off. By remembering and examining our dreams, we can gain a fuller understanding of ourselves and the issues of concern within a turning point.

In *Listening to Your Life*, Frederick Buechner writes:

Freudians and Jungians, prophets and poets, philosophers, fortune tellers and phonies all have their own claims about what dreams mean. Others claim they don't mean a thing. But there are at least two things they mean that seem incontrovertible. One of them is that through our dreams we are in constant touch with a world that is as real to us while we are in it, and has as much to do with who we are, and whose ultimate origin and destiny are as unknown and fascinating, as the world of waking reality. The other is that our lives are a great deal richer, deeper, more intricately interrelated, more mysterious and less limited by time and space than we commonly suppose.

From his study of 80,000 dreams during his long career as a psychoanalyst, Carl Jung believed that at the critical impasses in life, help does come from the profoundest depths of the psyche in dreams:

Dreams are an indispensable tool for self-knowledge. They are not "nothing but a dream." They are not freaks of nature and accidental. Rather they intend to advise, correct, punish, comfort, heal and warn the normal dreamer as much as they do the neurotic. Communication is their main purpose. They are a natural, spontaneous phenomenon and cannot be produced by an act of will or intellect nor can they be influenced by consciousness to tell something other than what they want to tell.

The dream speaks in images or pictures in a non-verbal, non-logical sensual language. The unconscious launches a dream to wake up the dreamer; to literally awaken him to some aspect of his conscious life or personal attitudes about which he is sound asleep.

There are multitudes of books and other resources available to you if you are interested in dream interpretation. Our belief, however, is that the only interpretation of any importance is your own. If you are not yet accustomed to remembering and finding meaning in your dreams, keep your journal next to your bed at night. When you awaken with a dream, take a few minutes to jot down your thoughts. Eventually you can train yourself to remember your dreams. Writing them down, however, can help you to recall details and record how you felt during your dream.

Your Spiritual Journey
There is so much cynicism and negativity surrounding life in America today, it's easy to feel discouraged and to feel somewhat hopeless. Our hope for you is that you find a comfortable space for spirituality in your life. It can also be helpful to find others who share your beliefs; whether it be organized religion, meditation groups, yoga classes, or even book clubs - wherever you feel your spiritual exploration will be supported, rather than judged. While some of us prefer personal spirituality, others find it a link to community. Finding the best fit for you and for spirituality in your life will help to move you forward in your goal of transition management.

Summary Points

- There is a rising interest in spirituality, both in traditional Western religions and the major religions of the East.
- Meditation and prayer can be learned by anyone.
- Meditation benefits physical and emotional health.
- Prayer is a way of soothing and healing your soul and accessing and enhancing your personal power.
- Your dreams can provide keys to your inner spiritual life.

Journal Subjects

- Describe your earliest memory of spirituality or religion. What impressions, images, or ideas about religion were you given by your family?
- How have these early experiences influenced the course of your life?
- Keep a dream record for at least two weeks. Are there any common themes?
- How would you describe your current spiritual health? What spiritual nourishment are you receiving now and what might you do to enhance it in the future?

Chapter 9

MAKING YOUR WORK LIFE YOUR LIFE'S WORK

"The fact is work is good for us. It demands activity, concentration, effort; it creates content and dreams; it keeps us in constant relationship with people. These dreams are all basic needs, the satisfaction of which gives us a sense of being alive. This feeling comes automatically with work."
— Allan Fromme

"This one step – choosing a goal and sticking to it – changes everything."
— Scott Reed

Take a minute to write down all of the words that come to mind when you think about the concept of work. Be sure to include the good, the bad, and the ugly. If you are like most people, then the bad and the ugly will usually have the most energy behind it (anger, frustration, sadness, disappointment, etc) and will create the longest list. Wouldn't it be fantastic if there was more positive energy (creativity, opportunity, joy, connectedness, success, fulfillment, etc) in our work lives?

Now, think about someone you know who seems to really enjoy their work. Who knows, it may even be someone at your current workplace. What is the difference between their connectedness and subsequent happiness with their work, and yours?

Work is the way in which we connect to the world in our culture. Think about it- work is always in the set of the first three questions people ask about you: *What's your name? What do you do?* or *What's your major?* Work is so important that those without specific job titles have difficulty in connecting with others and identifying themselves. Remember when "*domestic engineer*" and "*stay at home mom or dad*" replaced "*housewife*" as people began to question the idea that those without external employment didn't 'work' at all?

Over time, our expectations of the world of work have changed dramatically. It used to be that work was simply a means to an end - we work to support our family, or in order to do something else we enjoy. Now that we spend so much time at work and the boundaries between work and personal life have become so blurry, we expect work to provide intrinsic value. Work should be a source of happiness and fulfillment as well as a source of income. This notion, of course, is not a new one. Thomas Edison once said, "I never worked a day in my life. It was all fun." The difference now is that fulfillment and happiness at work used to be a seen as a gift, recognized for its rarity. Today we expect it. The incredibly high rate of turnover – a factor in the *new impermanence* - is fed by our constant search for something new, better, and more satisfying.

If you are currently struggling with a career transition, a professional turning point, then congratulations are in order. We congratulate you because you have choices. In fact, you are probably experiencing angst because there are so many choices, and the process is overwhelming. If you went into a bookstore and only three titles filled the shelves, it would be very easy to make a choice. You would read the descriptions and talk to the employees of the bookstore and simply decide which one was most interesting to you. Of course most bookstores contain thousands of books - more than you could ever review or ask about in a day. Which would you prefer? The three-book version is easier, isn't it?

Rewarding Work is Your Right

Over the years, working conditions have improved. Many of us have enough opportunities and education to make choices that allow us to do more than just survive. Indeed, the average worker looks to his employment for a sense of well-being, security and self-worth. Many of us find our work the most interesting part of our lives. We do more than work to live. Many of us live to work. Those of us who love our work are happy people.

MARK

Mark is a music teacher in an inner city school. He coaches the marching band and never misses a sports event. He also serves as advisor to the Youth Outreach Committee of the City Symphony. He works long hours in difficult conditions for a modest wage but he never complains – he considers himself lucky and loves what he does. He's the first to tell anyone, "I wouldn't trade my job for anything. I love kids, I love music and I love sports. I've got it made."

Of course, not everyone can be a music teacher and not everyone would find the career as fulfilling as Mark does. Why is that? Why would working as a high-power attorney eighty-plus hours a week appeal to some and seem completely ridiculous to others? Fulfilling, life-affirming careers are very personal. They connect who you are with what you do in a remarkable way.

Think about your favorite story. This could be a book, movie, play - just something that you could see or read over and over again. There are two things happening in that story that are important. First, there is the plot. The plot is what happened - the sequence of events that you could actually describe to other people. Second, there are the underlying themes that touch something inside you and make you feel connected to the story. The plot and the themes happen concurrently and the closer they are connected, the more poignant the story.

Careers work in the same way. Your plot is what you do on a daily basis - the actual tasks of your job. People who feel dissatisfied with their careers are not connected on a thematic level with their career plots. We may be very skilled at our positions and very successful in terms of advancement, praise, and salary, but who we are is so distant that we don't feel connected in any meaningful way.

EVERYONE deserves to do work that they connect to on a deep, personal level. While there may be periods of time in our lives when that is not possible for other reasons, in the grand scheme of things, everyone can make a choice to work in a way that is more reflective of their personal values.

The tricky part, of course, is figuring out what our personal themes are and then figuring out which of the vast opportunities out there will actually fit those themes. We also have the option of striking out on our own and creating opportunities unlike any others. As we've discussed throughout this book, the only way to manage your transitions more effectively is to know how to assess yourself and the world around you.

FRANCES

Frances worked her way through high school and college by selling dresses. When she graduated, she taught school for several years, moving from place to place as she followed her husband's career moves. When she was widowed at 35, she returned to college to study writing and eventually became a successful children's book writer. She then branched into business and real estate. For five years, she sold real estate, acted as marketing director for a development company and wrote about real estate while continuing to write for children. At fifty-seven, she started her fourth career as a minister of a church. She continues to write and teach as a part of her ministerial duties. She even uses the skills she learned in business to market the church and the religious books she now writes. When asked about her numerous career changes, she replied that she never changed careers - just collected new ones.

Creating Your Life's Work

What is the difference between the concept of "work life" and "life work"? The happy and successful person needs to have a positive attitude toward the many hours he or she spends in the world of work. It is not enough to love one's family and hate one's work. A well-balanced person will find a way to enjoy all of life. Let's face it: we'll spend more of our waking hours at work than anywhere else, and more time with colleagues than with loved ones.

Pursuing your life's work means you understand and are connected to what you do. It means you are *really* enjoying what you're doing - the challenges as well as the successes. We're talking about having a passion for your work. This is a feeling still foreign to most people, but it is incredibly important. The key has to do with your attitude: How do you approach what you do? This is a result of who you *are* and your perspective on life. No one likes every single aspect of their job. However, if you are doing your life's work - you have a sense of purpose for what you are doing - rather than just a job, the most mundane tasks take on a whole new aspect. Often, what we are doing doesn't matter if we believe the goal is meaningful. In other words, if we understand the *why* behind something, the *what* isn't as important.

It is sometimes difficult to figure out when it is time to instigate a turning point. Unlike the unexpected ones that catch us off guard, putting the energy into making a change can be monumental. First, ask yourself what percentage of your time at work or what percentage of your job you actually enjoy and feel fulfilled by.

Everyone has a different cut-off, but our advice is to follow the 80/20 rule. If you like your job more than eighty percent of the time, then you are probably in a good position. On the other hand, if you dislike your job more than twenty-percent of the time, you may be ready to get out. Second, think about a particularly bad day you had at work. When you think about it, would you say to yourself, "I hate my job," or "I hated today" or "I hated that situation." There is only a subtle difference between the first thought and the second two, but the distinction is VERY important. If you answered the first way then your dislike has been generalized or spread to your entire job. If your frustration is situation specific – limited to that day or that role - then it may be temporary or an isolated incident.

Because taking a risk to find something better means choosing between the known (I may not really like it, but at least its familiar) and the unknown (what if my next job is even worse?), you really need to take the time to manage your transition. If you decide to stay where you are, acknowledge that as a choice. Ignoring the decision is, by default, a choice too. As Will Rogers said, "Even if you're on the right track, you'll get run over if you just sit there."

The Five E's Formula for Lifework Success

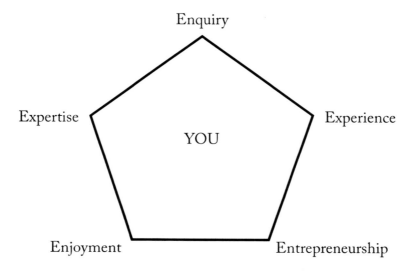

Enjoyment

Enjoyment provides the base because it is the key. In earlier chapters, you were asked to examine what you enjoy doing and being - what events and experiences you enjoyed the most and what personal qualities and personal values are most important to you. Your responses are the foundation for planning the directions in which your work life can expand. Of course, we also want you to remember the importance of balance. For example, we hope that enjoyment will include a commitment to achieve good relationships in your life.

Enjoyment is the basis for success in your life's work. However, there are many people who aren't sure just what work they most enjoy. No matter what you decide to try next, your attitude will mean everything. If you expect work to be boring and tiring, it will be. If you begin to believe that work can be fun, work will be fun.

Before you read on, in your journal take time-out to list five activities you have truly enjoyed in your life. Don't worry about the context - like whether you were paid or it was a class assignment or it was outside of work- just list and then describe them. Do they have anything in common? Does the list generate any new curiosities for you? Here is another tricky question: did you leave anything off of your list that popped into your brain because you thought it was silly or impractical? If so, add that to your list! After all, this is about *ENJOYMENT!*

Experience
Who and what you are has been shaped by your life experiences. In earlier chapters you have examined some of your experiences, attributes, strengths and values. You already know a great deal about yourself and your relationships with family, community and your commercial experiences, events and achievements. Generally, you can divide these into operational (things you've done) and administrative (things you've managed) experiences.

When looking at your experience in terms of your life's work, all of your accomplishments are relevant - including non-work activities. Take some time now to list experiences which you found particularly interesting, challenging, or otherwise successful. Then make a list of experiences that are memorable to you because you are proud of the way you handled or responded to a challenge. Remember that these experience stories could be about anything, including sports, education, artistic activities, family events, travel, group activities... anything! Record all of these stories in your journal.

Expertise
Until now, we have focused on your interests and those activities that give you great pleasure. These interests and activities certainly provide clues for designing your life's work, but you will also need skill or competency in order to flourish. Every individual has personal talents, capabilities and skills which set him or her apart from the group. Often, these attributes are undervalued because they come so

easily to the individual who possesses them. The question is, "what do you naturally do well?"

You want to be sure you know what your special skills are and how you have demonstrated them. These are attributes that you can do well - as demonstrated by your accomplishments. In addition to a list you create yourself, you will also want to enlist feedback from others - close friends, siblings, parents, kids - to really get a sense of what others value in you. In addition, there may be other skills you think you may have which have not been developed or demonstrated yet. Definitely identify these if you think they would be enjoyable. Continue to use your journal or your online assessments and list all those that are relevant.

Enquiry
Now that you have a better understanding of what you have to offer the world, you'll need to start exploring how it all fits together with someone else's needs. Whether you think of that as how you will contribute to the world or just one employer, understanding they way it all fits together is how you will begin to turn your talents into a marketable product.

This step is crucial to the validity of the *five "E"* formula because it asks you to be curious about new questions like;

- What do I have to offer that the world needs?
- What does my set of abilities offer that my employer (or client) needs, wants and will pay for?
- What are the opportunities for me to continue my personal and career growth?
- Where are the business or social needs that provide growth opportunities?
- How do I discover how and where I might find the best fit?

True enquiry requires more than just making a list of attributes and possible answers to random questions. Often, it is a long term investigation which includes numerous sources. Some of these may include library research, online career exploration, a part time internship, or informational interviewing. Ask questions, observe and, if possible, hang around long enough to see if the work you are considering suits you. Often there is a great disparity between perception about a particular occupation and the actual activity. Observing that career can help give you a much more accurate picture.

MICHELLE

Michelle had a degree in nursing, but she became bored of routine hospital work and began considering a move to hospice nursing. She was drawn to the idea of helping people die well. She saw it as spiritually fulfilling as well as physically helpful and she hoped she would find it more meaningful than her present work. After discussions with several hospice nurses, she discovered that their days were spent mostly on paper work and forms. She decided to look outside the field of nursing for something completely different and more spiritually oriented. She eventually entered a seminary and later the ministry.

It is important to approach the step of enquiry seriously and make a thorough investigation of any change you are considering. Check out the requirements, the opportunities, the hours and working conditions, the pay, the opportunities for advancement and the satisfaction level of people who are currently doing the sort of work you are considering. Good investigation creates solid decisions and happy lives. Too many unhappy people dream of romantic occupations without checking the facts.

JANET

Janet was working in retail and wanted to move to a new job with a less demanding and more regular work schedule. After some general investigation and self-study, she began extensive reading on the appraisal field and the marketing of antiques. She interviewed several people in the business, all of whom were happy to talk to her because she posed interesting questions. Then she enrolled in a local college and took courses in appraisal. Her preparation for her new career was based on some clever investigation, a strong interest and a logical approach. Her career change has been successful.

Even if you are strongly attracted to making a change, you may want to do it in stages. Many people begin a new business or career by operating part time until they have achieved a safer financial status or have developed their confidence enough to approach their new work full time. Part time beginnings have the extra advantage of giving you a chance to test the water.

Remember that gratification is not always instantaneous. The fruits of your labor may not materialize for some time. Because of financial and other considerations, it may not always be feasible for you to reach the pinnacle of your life's work right away. Remember the *new longevity*. You will maintain confidence about your long-term success in small, manageable short-term steps.

Entrepreneurship
This fifth "E" is a matter of attitude. In the new reality of a changing workplace with little long-term company connection, you must learn to think like a free agent. While it is important to investigate and make your decisions based on the best information you can gather, it is also important to move in the direction of your dreams. Do your homework and trust your instinct. You can't just sit back on your heels and expect the world to come to you. To take charge of your life with energy and enthusiasm, you must function productively, diplomatically, thoughtfully, patiently, purposefully, and joyfully.

Taking Risks
If you are going to design a life based on your dreams, you are probably going to have to take some risks. There comes a time when the only sensible move is to take a risk!

RALPH

Although he loved his job, Ralph could see that the future of his position was in jeopardy. His company had merged with another and it was apparent that some duplicate positions would be eliminated. Throughout his life, Ralph had been a clever inventor - often using tools in his garage to create new solutions to little problems. One such invention was a tool used with shrimp. He decided to produce and package this shrimp tool and then spent his weekends marketing the product at grocery stores. By the time he was downsized, Ralph had enough momentum behind his new business that he was able to move to that on a full-time basis.

There are many people out there who have great skills and ideas but don't want to risk the security of full-time employment with benefits. Ralph's story provides a great example of how you can begin to explore new opportunities without much risk. In a sense, it is like dipping a toe in the water rather than jumping from the high dive! Of course some new adventures require an "all or nothing" approach, but many do not.

TERRY

Terry had a good job as a communications specialist in a library, but she had always dreamed of owning her own landscaping company. She decided to take a small step toward her dream by enrolling in weekend classes. After two years she had all the necessary credentials to be a landscape designer. She started her job search and was finally able to make the transition from it being a hobby to work by quitting her library job and going to work for a well-known local landscaper. After working with them for five years in various positions, she was able to save enough money to strike out on her own. Although it didn't happen overnight, Terry's journey and transition from communication specialist to owning her own landscape business was enjoyable and she ended up in her life's work.

Summary Points

- You now have the opportunity to design your work life so that it is rewarding in many ways- so that it becomes your life's work.
- You can design your work life based on what you enjoy, your expertise and your experience.
- Intelligent <u>enquiry</u> is an absolute necessity before you make a move.
- There is often a need to take a risk if you are to design a life work which suits your individual desires and talents.
- By assessing your comfort level with risk, you can take steps that feel manageable to you.

Journal Subjects

- Ask three friends to describe your most outstanding skills and talents. Create a composite portrait of yourself based on their assessment.
- Write a letter of recommendation for yourself for a "dream" job. Describe why you are perfect for it. Have fun with this one.
- Be sure you have completed your five work-type activities you truly enjoyed.
- Be sure you have completed your list of several accomplishments that you truly enjoyed and are proud of the work you did.

Chapter 10

TAKING CHARGE OF YOUR LIFE & WORK

"To find a career to which you are adapted by nature, and then to work hard at it, is about as near to a formula for success and happiness as the world provides. One of the fortunate aspects of this formula is that, granted the right career has been found, the hard work takes care of itself. Then hard work is not hard work at all."

- Mark Sullivan

One of the most important ingredients in a well-lived life is an attitude of being in charge. Most people think of the word "entrepreneur" as referring to a small business owner or someone who starts any business operation and takes risks. It is equally applicable to corporate or government workers anywhere. It doesn't matter a bit whether you are working for your father-in-law, a multinational corporation, the U.S. government or in business for yourself; crucial to your success is your understanding of your role as a "free agent". Whether you get a paycheck from an employer or a client, your career success is solely dependent on you.

The term *"preneurship"* describes this attitude. The usual prefix associated with this word -*entrepreneurship*- and the traditional translation includes both an attitude and an investment. Of course, the investment can be in time or money, or both. Literally, the word *entrepreneurship* means: "begin to take charge." In this context, it is an invitation to take charge of your life, your career, and your well-being.

A number of years ago, as part of an informal "think tank" group exploring the role of spiritual values in business, management consultant Gifford Pinchot coined the term "*intra-preneurship.*" He later wrote a popular book entitled *Intrapreneuring* and the term began to be used to encourage entrepreneurial attitudes within companies, especially in the high tech sector. Companies such as Xerox and 3M have adopted intrapreneurial strategies and structures in order to encourage creative development of new products.

Another form of the root word could be *inter-preneurship*. This is behavior typical of task or project teams that constructively operate across functional and operational lines, taking charge in the larger interest of the enterprise as a whole. This is also reflected in the team approach to organizational structure, which is very common in companies today.

Finally, there is the aspect of *inner-preneurship*, which can be used to describe the gift of an examined life or taking charge of what is inside oneself. Implicit in this term is the recognition that you can become self-directed in the management of your career, health and financial issues. All you need is to know yourself well and how to connect yourself to the evolving needs of employers, clients, and the community, in other words: how to self-manage your transitions. In the spirit of *preneurship,* you can take control and be prepared for any turning point whether anticipated, intentional or involuntary.

- *Entrepreneurship* -- taking charge of your own business
- *Intrapreneurship* -- taking charge within a business
- *Interpreneurship* -- taking charge within your group
- *Innerpreneurship* -- taking charge of your own life

Application of the *five E's formula* and the principle of *preneurship* are essential components for successfully navigating career transitions at any age. Career turning points start early in life and most working adults experience these transitions over and over again as they grow. If transitions are taken lightly without much thought, they will be a constant source of confusion and frustration throughout your lifetime. With all the changes coming so fast, the need for a thorough examination of your life and goals from time to time becomes more important than ever. External situations everywhere are more and more complex. We can't even begin to anticipate what new developments will change our lives in the next ten, twenty, or thirty years. You do not, however, have to just sit back and react to changes as they come. If you are prepared, then you will be able to respond more quickly to your turning points - and with more authority. This means becoming proactive and keeping your eyes open. Create a vision and a plan and take charge of your life!

Your vision should include your own personal definition of success and happiness. Within the context of transition management, success means navigating life's turning points in a way that feels comfortable and satisfying to you. It is a way of living rather than an end result. With a new vision of future goals beyond yourself comes a feeling of making your future count, feeling good, and having in mind who you are, what your most important relationships are, and how your experiences help you to meet your goals and give your life meaning.

Any turning point presents an exciting opportunity because of the challenges that go along with it. Turning points offer you the chance for a *breakthrough* to new ground, new awareness, new attitudes and new behaviors.

Turning Point: School to Work
In today's world, most young people acquire some sort of technical training or attend college after graduating from high school. The first career turning point is selecting a college or technical school. That selection can be crucial in some cases. In others, it is simply a choice based on limited opportunities or funds.

The second important turning point is selecting a major. As happens with most other significant turning points, the process of selecting a major is laden with myths and assumptions. Some students believe that selecting a major automatically means selecting a career. Others feel that they are rejecting all other opportunities by selecting just one major. Still others believe if they don't choose the "right" major, they may never find the "right" career. In fact, there is no direct relationship between major and career. True, some majors are more vocational in nature and tend to prepare students for certain professions, but most are designed as general starting points with a particular specialization. Usually when a student is completely anxiety-ridden about his or her choice of major, they have the idea that what he or she selects that day will be what they will have to do for the next fifty-sixty years! While this is true in other countries, in the U.S. our reality is much different. After graduation, your major may or may not have any relationship to the career you end up pursuing.

Make a list of significant others in your life. Next to their names, note their college majors and their current career fields or job titles. You will probably notice that while some people are still working in the same field, many are in careers completely unrelated to their major. College is about becoming an educated person; a person who can think critically and problem-solve creatively. Those skills are valuable just about anywhere, regardless of the major you choose. If you are currently trying to choose a major, RELAX. This is a manageable transition in a certain direction, but your direction can be changed later.

Once a student's formal education is completed, the number of choices can be overwhelming. Depending on the amount of freedom available when selecting a school, deciding what to do after graduation can be the first real decision-point for most students. With little guidance and no experience, many young people are overwhelmed at the prospect of finding their first job, let alone finding rewarding and successful life work.

The simple truth is that most young people completing high school, college, or graduate school find the world of work a total mystery. They may have helped pay for their education with part time jobs. They may have taken a year or two off at one time and worked, but they are often innocent about the world of work. The truth is that these people have marketable skills and can be successful if they would only take a moment to stop and think about what they have to offer.

Perhaps the most dramatic transition at this point in human development is one from dependent to independent. Most college students continue to be supported by their parents and have numerous resources on campus to help them navigate life. By design, graduation from college marks the transition into independence. While we may not expect new graduates to immediately marry and start having children anymore, we tend to hope they will start moving in a professional direction.

It is tempting for students transitioning from school to work to allow someone (like their parents) to make decisions or manage this turning point for them. At no time is the temptation stronger than during this time - one of life's great turning points. We hope if you are a young man or woman just starting out in the world of work, that you will adopt a proactive, *preneurial* attitude quickly. It is important to accept your power and take responsibility for your own future. We know it is possible, and the sooner you start, the better you will get at managing transitions, and the happier you will be.

Turning Point: Early Career
We all know someone who trained for one career but never worked in that field. Sometimes the switch seemed to be dependent on outside conditions, but often it is the result of an earlier turning point.

MARVIN

By the time he finished law school, Marvin knew that he was going to hate practicing law. As graduation drew near, the promised job in his fiancée's family firm really began to look like a prison sentence. Although he loved his girlfriend, he really wanted to run away from the life they'd mapped out. On the day after his graduation, he broke his engagement and took a bus to a new town where there were no expectations. After a few occasions of drinking too much and attempts at surviving on a minimum wage, he landed a job on a small business newspaper. Within two years, he had a job at a city newspaper where he covered the courthouse. Eventually, he and his girlfriend were reunited and married – on their own terms.

While he has never actually practiced law, his education was paramount in helping him to get his position and in helping him understand the cases he covers.

Usually, people have to try their chosen careers for a while until they reach a turning point. Rob changed his mind about his career six years after he got out of college.

ROB

Rob found a great job out of college through his campus career center. After working there about a year, he decided that he had learned what he could from that career. He became bored and felt that he hadn't reached his earning potential. He decided to return to school to advance his marketable education. Unlike his undergraduate experience, which felt somewhat disconnected from the world, his graduate school experience felt much more connected to his life and work. Upon his second graduation, he took a technical engineering job in a large industrial company; then he switched to a small family-owned commodity trading company. He did well but advancement was limited. Rob then moved up by switching to similar work in a large multinational firm. At age 42, he was asked by the firm to take on new business development responsibilities and move to another city.

By carefully assessing his work situations and anticipating changes, Rob was able to make calculated changes to advance his career. Unlike thirty years ago when frequent job change was seen as negative, Rob's self-management showed his employers that he was a savvy planner who knew how to execute a mission.

Rob is an example of someone who began a professional career right out of school. Many people do not know what to do after graduation and spend some time "finding themselves" before moving to a professional position or going back to graduate school.

KATHY

Kathy graduated from a small liberal arts college in the Midwest. While she did not know exactly what she wanted to do, she did know that she wanted it to be different than the life she had become accustomed to. When she graduated, she decided to try life in a big city, get a job, and room with a couple of college classmates. She tried various things for a career - clerical jobs, waiting tables, and telemarketing for a brokerage firm- but nothing seemed to fit. Frustrated by a lack of professional options, she decided to pursue a path to prestige and go to law school.

She enjoyed law school, graduated, and passed her bar exam on the first try. She got a good job with a downtown firm and worked for two years. To her great sorrow, she found that she was just as unhappy in law as she had been doing the menial jobs she had before.

She finally sought help from a career counselor. She stopped to examine her life seriously for the first time and experienced a breakthrough. She gained an understanding of herself and the situations in which she had been operating, and came to terms with why she didn't seem to fit. She also rediscovered a passion she hadn't really thought about since grade school - a basic enjoyment for math and quantitative problem-solving. While her previous attempts at jobs had involved people, she found most comfort and enjoyment in analyzing numbers.

Kathy decided to combine her interests and her training to pursue a specialization in tax law. She found a mentor in her firm and managed to successfully transition into that area. Now she is satisfied and successful at work.

Turning Point: Mid-Career

Most everyone has heard of a mid-life crisis, right? You realize you are getting older, quit your job, have an affair and buy a sports car. That's the stereotype. Although it is hard to define mid-life or mid-career anymore, the underlying questions that cause that kind of crisis occur to most of us at some point. Is this it? Am I happy? Is this all there is to life? Am I going to do this until I die? Is it too late to change direction? Isn't there more to life than this? This type of crisis is the essence of a turning point. These questions underlie what we do every single day. If we suppress them and say "I'll think about it later," then they will most likely reemerge in dramatic and painful ways. If, on the other hand, we are always thinking about our next step, about what more we want to give and receive, then the emotions never reach crisis.

PEGGY AND FRANK

When Frank finished college, he joined his family's small clothing manufacturing business –first in finance to learn the operation and then in marketing to learn about their customers. Even though Frank had an inside track to the top, he decided that he wanted to find out if he could make it on his own. A college friend had told him about an opportunity in the federal government in Washington, D.C, and he leapt at the chance. After a few years, he shifted careers once again when another friend asked him to join a real estate development and management company, where he advanced to become its chief operating officer.

While Frank was moving from field to field, Peggy was working in marketing, her college major. When Frank took a position in a new location, Peggy looked at companies comparable to her own and usually had no trouble finding a new position. Although she considered herself successful, Peggy sometimes felt that she would have advanced more quickly had she been able to stay with a particular company for a longer period of time. She began to feel resentful of Frank's wanderings and felt that he was being selfish.

At the age of 45, Frank declared that he needed a change. He wasn't satisfied, and felt that he wasn't moving any closer to his goals. Peggy, on the other hand, had finally reached her goal of senior partner and decided that she didn't want to make another move. Both Frank and Peggy had arrived at a turning point. Using journals and some of the activities presented in this book, they started to note and articulate their own goals, both independently and as a couple. Both took the time to step back and get a bigger view of their accomplishments, successes, skills, and experiences as well as the frustrations.

While Frank was exploring his personal life and his life's work, his company was also changing. In fact, the Board of Directors asked him to analyze their organizational structure and find ways to maximize efficiency by streamlining the operation. Frank followed the same method for analyzing the company as he had himself. His final conclusion was that the company was top heavy and he proposed a new management structure that did not include him. He negotiated a fair yet lucrative severance package, which gave him the flexibility to make a new start.

Although Frank never considered its potential for a "real" career, he had always enjoyed music as a hobby. He often talked about doing more in the industry when he retired. As he was transitioning out of his company position, he met a person coordinating a local music festival. Having free time, Frank was able to assist. He quickly realized that his business experience and leadership skills, combined with a passion for music, would easily fit into this career field. Rather than waiting for retirement or that magical "some day" to do what he actually wanted to do, he seized the opportunity to begin working in the music business.

Frank's turning points also brought about changes in his relationship with Peggy. He had often felt envious of her ability to find her life's passion so early in her career. On the other hand, she felt that she had always been expected to sacrifice her own career advancement whenever Frank made a transition to something new. Once they began to talk about the way in which they wanted to live, they were able to clear the air of bad feelings on both sides. By Frank's creating a new career path locally, Peggy wasn't put into a position of having to choose between his career happiness and hers. By practicing the art of preneurship –taking charge of their lives and articulating a shared vision– they feel confident and prepared to handle whatever comes.

Frank and Peggy's story is a perfect example of the success that is possible when people take a little time in the middle of their lives to examine the bits and pieces of their lives and get a picture of what has and has *not* happened so far. Re-examining your life has never been more important. Today's world of multiple companies, multiple professions like Frank's, multiple jobs - in some cases, multiple wives and husbands, and children - means that changes will be coming in your life. Instead of feeling adrift and vulnerable to every new wave or breeze that comes, having a solid sense of self and mission will help you feel more in control.

There are the exceptional lucky few whose work continues to be forever challenging - with continuing personal growth and opportunity on the job. At some point, most people begin to get a little bored. This is probably because they aren't continuing to grow, learn, and be challenged. You could be one of those feeling the need to re-charge your batteries. If you are feeling that way, take charge. You have a long life and a long career ahead of you. If you are physically and mentally healthy, you've got many good career years ahead of you. You are much wiser now than you were fifteen or twenty years ago when you first entered the world of work. Make sure all that time and experience counts for something valuable for you. Take a minute to get your bearings. It is NEVER too late to do something new - even if it involves more education or starting at the beginning of a new field. The choice is yours. Gather the information you need regarding yourself and your choices and make an informed, exciting choice.

Turning Point: Retirement/Recreation

Like everything else we've discussed in this book, the concept of retirement is much different now than it used to be. Formerly, one of the only career fields in which people retired and regularly went on to completely different careers was the military. Now people are "retiring" all the time. They may move directly on to a new career, take time off from work, or may begin volunteering or working without pay.

Perhaps the word "retirement" is outdated. When viewing this period of time as a turning point, a better word may be recreation. At its heart, recreation involves just that - creating oneself all over again. The original concept of Turning Points was geared specifically towards this group of people. We noticed that many people encounter the retirement turning point completely unprepared, and the results can be disastrous. As people retired from careers that served as their major identity markers, retirees lost their sense of self, leading to marital problems, illness, and sometimes death. If what you do is all you are and you don't find another way to express that after you retire, what do you have left?

Recreation, on the other hand, can be a tremendous opportunity to grow and contribute in new and exciting ways. Assessing who you are, where you've been, and how you contribute to the world can help you define your mission as in any other transition. Finding meaning and connecting with your life themes will help you to make a positive turning point.

Transition Management

The stories in this chapter indicate the breakthroughs that can occur - and how the turning points in your life can work *for* you rather than take you by surprise or destroy your life. Although most of these experiences started with trouble, these people moved through their rough spots. They had breakthroughs.

If you are at a place where you need to move through some trouble and find a breakthrough of your own, remember that you can do it. You can have a breakthrough because this kind of experience is available to anyone willing to look at his or her life honestly and make some changes. Opportunity for a new kind of success is available to anyone, regardless of generation or income status. Have a vision, name your mission, and then have the determination and courage to take it seriously. Then don't just wish for your vision to become a reality, but put energy into making it come true. No matter how much people love you, they will not do it for you - you are the only one who can. Know that you have a long life ahead of you and that all things are possible if you have the courage to take charge.

Summary Points

- Our first career turning points often occur as we select training programs or higher education, as well as educational majors.
- Some people encounter sharp career turning points very early while others make more gradual turns.
- Stereotypical mid-life crises are psychological stages based not on age but life circumstances. Viewed as turning points, they are important opportunities for growth.
- Retirement or a move towards recreation is just another turning point, not an ending.

Journal Subjects

- Write a few paragraphs about your very first job. What did you discover about yourself? Were there conflicts or turning points involved? Are those conflicts resolved?
- Examine the way your work life is related to your family life. How do you set priorities? Would you like to change anything?
- What career turning points have you experienced so far? After you've listed them, indicate how much control you felt over that transition on a scale of 1-10 with one being no control and ten being total control. Are there any patterns to the difference? In retrospect, what could you have done differently?

Chapter 11

CHART YOUR ADVENTURE

*"As yesterday is history, and tomorrow may never come, I have resolved
from this day on, I will do all the business I can honestly, have all the
fun I can reasonably, do all the good I can willingly ."*
-Robert Louis Stevenson

Just as today is the first day of the rest of your life, so today is your
chance to begin to electrify your work life in the direction of your
life's work. The time to begin is now and the place to begin is right
where you are. Rather than taking an enormous leap somewhere, we
are asking that you start with a small, manageable step in the right
direction.

One important concept to understand is that whatever activity you
choose deserves your full energy and effort. If you are painting the
fence, paint it with all your passion. If you are writing a report,
playing the flute, raking leaves or conducting a meeting, your choice
of work deserves your full attention and enthusiasm. No matter
what the job is, it is a chance to practice a *preneurial* attitude.

Never allow yourself to slip into a passive role. Just letting life happen
to you is like lying in the middle of the road and hoping not to get
hit by a car. Passivity is an easy habit to fall into. It destroys peace
of mind. No day can be longer than a day in which you just wait for

things to come down the hall and slap you around. If the work is worthy of you, then do it with enthusiasm. If it isn't worth doing, find something else that is. Your attitude is vitally important to your opportunities and your attitude will control your destiny. Former Mobil Oil CEO Lou Noto described his philosophy this way:

At the end of the day, what separates platitudes and preaching from success and performance? Two things: commitment and passion. You've got to love what you do. You've got to be in it. And if you don't feel for it, you should get out and do something else.

I started with Mobil 36 years ago, and it seems like yesterday. Time goes by quickly, and if you aren't spending it on things that really turn you on, then you should find something else that does. I get criticized a lot within Mobil because that's what I tell my people. If you're not willing to play, if you're not willing to feel that this is your hardware store, then find a new career. A lot of people find that harsh. But I think its good advice for living.

While it is true that people are sometimes given unfair advantage for one reason or another, it is more often true that the good worker gets the promotion. Even if it is a temporary job or one you know you will be leaving, you never know how a solid experience now will help you in the future. Maintaining your integrity in the workplace is crucial if you plan to be happy in your work life.

ANNE, SALLY AND JIM

Three young people apply for jobs as checkers in the local grocery store. They are all turned down because of lack of experience, but they are all offered jobs bagging groceries and helping people to their cars. The first young woman, Anne, turns the job down because it is only minimum wage and she wants to save for a trip to St. Louis. The second two take the job and one of them, Jim, works very hard. The second one, Sally, talks a lot and takes as many breaks as she can. By the end of the month, Anne is still looking for a job and Sally is still bagging, but Jim has been promoted to checker. Their fate was decided by their attitude.

Developing a proactive attitude can begin immediately. You do not need to wait until you finish reading this book, nor do you need to have it all figured out before you begin to do your best. People who delay working hard until they find work they like almost never achieve their goals. Hard work provides both tangible and intangible rewards.

Without a direction, however, hard work will not be enough. After all, if you row as hard as you can on one side of the boat, you'll only go in a circle. It takes balance to move forward. To achieve your goals, you need to know where you want to go, and chart your course carefully in order to get there. You have started to get to know yourself. You have thought about the people who are important in your life. You have been introduced to the concept of your life's work and the art of *preneurship*. You have an appreciation for the world of change and uncertainty and you know this is the world where you are choosing career and job opportunities.

Now that you've gathered all of this information, you need to start organizing it in a way that is meaningful for you. If you think of this next step as a new adventure, then this planning stage is one of plotting your course. Your adventure brings with it a renewed focus on your personal interests. Specifically, it puts the spotlight on what you want and on what resources you have or will need in order to get it.

MY WANTS
Our wants break down into three categories:

Category 1: What do I want to <u>Have</u>?
While we could be lofty and say that material things aren't important, the truth of the matter is that most of us work to be able to have certain things. Many of us say things like, "I don't need to be rich, I just want to be comfortable." If that is true for you, then you need to ask yourself exactly what "comfortable" means. Using your journal or online tools, make a list of everything you might like to have - cars, boats, houses, clothes, longer weekends, more children, more friends, more travel, sports equipment, theater tickets - get it all out in the open where you can see it. Don't be realistic, be indulgent! This is your wish list- the material things you WANT from life.

Category 2: What do I want to <u>Do</u>?

For many people, this category is composed of two parts: career interests and personal interests. These parts may be connected to material desires. There is really just one criterion applicable - what do you (or would you) *enjoy* doing? If you are happy with your work you have probably already taken charge. If you'd like to change, you've already been pushed into a change, or if you'd like to expand or enhance existing interests, write down specifics.

What sorts of things are you curious about? In your daily routine, what are the things you enjoy doing? Most people have more than one endeavor they find satisfying. Some people have dreams about some project or job for which there is never enough time or the circumstances are wrong. Without second-guessing yourself, include every conceivable work life interest that might appeal to you, whether or not you presently have the knowledge, experience or expertise to do it.

Apply the same thought process to personal, family, community and recreational interests. After making these lists off the top of your head, you may wish to rearrange items in terms of priorities such as short term or long term goals. You may also wish to go beyond a word or phrase and indicate in depth just exactly what you mean.

Category 3: What do I want to <u>Be</u>?

It is important to answer this question both as an individual person, and in relationship to the outside world. What kind of person do you aspire to be? Is your day-to-day behavior consistent with your personal values? Are your attitudes toward your quality of life constructive? Do you want to be self-responsible, entrepreneurial; a person of principle? Find words to describe those personal and lifestyle qualities that are important to you and that characterize what you enjoy about yourself and your world. Again, be spontaneous; don't evaluate until later.

Now it's time to prioritize all your wants. This needs to be done both within each of the three categories, and - item by item - among the three. Where there are connections between what you want to do and what you want to be - it'll be necessary to think about them together.

MY RESOURCES – IN HAND AND NEEDED

What resources do I need to get what I want? The next step in charting your next move requires an analysis of the <u>Knowledge</u>, <u>Experience</u>, <u>Expertise</u> and <u>Relationships</u> areas. This analysis will help you identify those resources you have in hand and those you need to obtain. You need to make specific linkages between resources required and the wants to be satisfied. Much of what you require you probably already have; other elements may be missing.

Category 4: What <u>Experiences</u> Do I Need?

Link the past accomplishments you identified earlier with your goals. Now, what additional experiences do you need to get what you want? Can they be accomplished on your own or do you need to be part of a group or organization? You will need a post-it for each experience. Reference each one to its associated *Have, Do* or *Be* item.

Category 5: What <u>Expertise</u> Do I need?

Review your capabilities list. Identify key skills that you already have that relate to what you want. Pick out other skills you could develop further. At this time, you will probably think of capabilities you need which would be new to you. Highlight those that you enjoy most or expect to enjoy in the future. Each skill or personal quality pertinent to your *Have, Do* or *Be* items should have its own post-it and should reference one or more "Wants."

Category 6: What <u>Knowledge</u> Do I Need?

Retraining and relearning on a regular basis is going to be essential in the new millennium. Science and technology are going to continue to demand back-to-school time. As you ponder what you need to know in order to get what you want, continued learning is likely to link very quickly to many if not all of your priority "Wants." Identify priority knowledge requirements and interests and post each item, linking it to priority "Wants."

Category 7: What <u>Relationships</u> Do I Need?

Hardly anything can be accomplished on your own. You need support from professionals, peers, family and friends. You may need to network extensively to discover hidden opportunities to apply your expertise, experience and knowledge. Once again, on post-its, identify key people you know (or to whom you could gain access) who could provide information and resources to help meet your needs.

Mission

Up to this point, we've asked you to expand - expand your self-awareness, your network, and your knowledge of work. While it would be nice if you could continue this exploration and expansion stage forever, your current turning point may require you to start narrowing down. Good transition management includes understanding this expansion and narrowing pattern. Its like breathing in and out - the lungs expand and let everything in, then they contract and push out what is no longer needed at the moment. Managing your turning points requires the same give and take.

At this point in the book, stop and take a deep breath. Read what you've written in your journal or online exercises so far and highlight the particularly poignant parts. If you've gone through this book systematically, you should have a great deal of information to sort through. Are there any themes emerging? Do you see any patterns?

A mission statement is one way to synthesize and clarify what you've learned about yourself and how you want to interact with and contribute to the world. In the new reality of the world of work, people with more success tend to have goals that align directly with their organizations' goals. Average workers simply absorb the mission of others, while above-average workers understand the connectedness of personal and professional mission. Taking the time to consider, write, and revise your mission helps to connect what you are doing with who you are as a person. Having a mission can also help you to make decisions in times of transition - it is a measuring stick against which you can measure choices. Finally, it gives you an overall structure for guiding your branding, job searches, resumes, cover letters, and interviews. Michael Goodman described the value of a mission statement by defining it as, "*an articulation of what you're all about and what success looks like to you.*"

Take some time to think about and write a mission statement. It can be general or specific, short or long, personal or professional. We aren't talking about a slogan, catch phrase, or goal, we are talking about a statement that characterizes who you are and how you want to be.

In one of his sermons, Dr. Ralph Ahlberg, a UCC minister, said it so well: "*Having a meaning and purpose in our lives is our number one need. If we don't have any sense of meaning, if we can't point to any purpose beyond our narrowly defined self-interest, all the power and prestige in the world will still leave us hollow and incomplete.*"

Commit yourself to something worthy
Until one is committed there is hesitancy, the chance to draw back, always ineffectiveness. Concerning all acts of initiative (and creation), there is one elementary truth, the ignorance of which kills countless ideas and splendid plans: that the moment one definitely commits oneself, then Providence moves too. All sorts of things occur to help one that would otherwise never have occurred. A whole stream of events issues from the decision, raising in one's favor all manner of unforeseen incidents and meetings and material assistance, which no man could have dreamt, would have come his way. I have learned a deep respect for one of Goethe's couplets: "Whatever you can do, or dream you can . . . begin it. Boldness has genius, power and magic in it."

-W.N. Murray

Summary Points

- Make a habit of your best possible work ethic.
- Commit to a purpose in your life.
- Write your mission statement and revise it often.

Journal Subjects

- What is your mission in life?
- What is your life purpose?
- How do your work plans fit into that purpose?

Chapter 12

BRANDING YOURSELF

"There is a product. You are the product. Your values, priorities, skills, experience, even your high and low tolerances, represent a combination some prospective buyer will find very attractive. You are the solution to that buyer's needs."

– Burton & Wedemeyer

You are always working for yourself, whether or not you are the one who signs your paycheck. In this fast changing world, it is important to understand that no other individual or any organization can possibly be responsible for managing you or your career as effectively as you can do it yourself.

Each of us must be in charge of every aspect of our lives. We must plan for our own financial security because we can't count on company retirement systems in a world obsessed with downsizing. We must be in charge of our own career enhancement education because current ways of doing things and current technologies may be obsolete tomorrow. So we must constantly upgrade our skills and learn new ones. Perhaps most important of all, we must be in charge of marketing ourselves as workers, not just when we are unemployed, but all of the time.

TIM

Tim worked as a computer programmer for seven years. Since he enjoyed travel and his two colleagues did not, he was often on the road. He and his family planned to stay right where they were. Then the company was sold and Tim was suddenly out of a job. Fortunately, he had contacts all over the nation. He got on the telephone and within one week had three offers. Each offer involved a move and a pay raise. Looking back, Tim says, "It was a 'good news and bad news' situation but I'm really grateful my job allowed me to make so many friends in the industry. A lot of the other people are still looking".

Be sure your good work is recognized

In effect, each one of us is responsible for being his or her own public relations agency. We need to approach our efforts as though we were marketing ourselves as a commodity in the work place. To be effective in today's work world, we need to be constantly aware of our marketing tactics, even if we have no plans to change jobs.

A good public relations program makes sure you get credit for your good works. It is not aimed at deceiving anyone or tearing anyone else down, it is simply designed to make sure those who can influence your future know the best there is to know about you. It can be low key, natural and courteous. The worker who hides his or her light under a blanket of false modesty is often overlooked. You don't have to shout but make sure your chosen target audience hears about you and your accomplishments.

Your target audience may be influential people in your field, potential employers, your present employer or your current supervisor. Even if you have no intention of ever leaving your present position, a good public relations program is in order. Remember that the traditional definition of public relations is "getting credit for the good you are doing." It is simply not enough to be a good worker. Make sure you get credit for being a good worker.

Most people spend many hours each week on their work life. Many have elaborate schemes for setting priorities to get the job done most efficiently. Very, very few people understand how important it is to their success to market themselves continuously.

JUDY

After a fifteen-year time out to raise a family, Judy was hired as an office-based advertising person at her town newspaper. When she was hired, her supervisor mentioned that she was overqualified for the position and suggested she might apply for one of the outside sales positions when there was a vacancy. She told the supervisor she would be very interested and wanted the job. Although she was a good worker, she was passed over for two outside sales positions the first year. In both cases, the jobs were filled by people who were younger and more aggressive. Judy felt she was being passed over because of her age but she agreed to undertake a program to market herself more effectively, specifically selecting her supervisor as her target. She made it a point to let him know when she did something special at work. She also let him know about her volunteer activities. When she was elected President of her Women's Club, she sent her photo in with the news clipping. Her supervisor actually put the newspaper story on the lunch room bulletin board. She was the only candidate interviewed for the next opening and she got the job.

Some people are able to "sell" themselves easily and naturally. They possess a knack for being noticed. The rest of us have to cultivate this skill to make sure our name gets on the program when we work long hours on the committee. Be sure to put your name on the papers you write or the (constructive) suggestions you make.

TOM

Tom is a free-lance writer who often works on team projects. Tom learned several years ago that he needed to negotiate money, deadlines and writing credits if he was going to be a successful writer. He tells this story, "I had a job writing a script for a small production company and the director sent out a press release claiming he had written the script. When I complained, he said it was too late now. That same year, I sold some short stories to an educational anthology some professor was putting together. When the book came out, her name was on the jacket cover as editor and writer and my name was nowhere to be found. That was fifteen years ago and I've been very careful to claim credit in advance since then."

An intelligent marketing program is always aimed at the prospective customer. Sometimes it is very effective to be in a visible position, such as team leader. Sometimes it is even more effective to be behind the scenes, helping those in power take the credit. There are times when working on the sidelines pays off and times when it is important to be out front. An employee who is able to spot needs or problems and make sure they are solved before they are noticed needs to make sure that his or her talents are acknowledged.

Document your successes and accomplishments
As a matter of habit, you should keep all letters of commendation and official recognition. In addition, throw in copies of informal notes and emails saying you've done a good job. There are times when it may be appropriate to ask someone who gives a verbal compliment to put it in writing. Don't be shy about forwarding copies of favorable comments about you to your boss.

You should develop a systematic networking procedure and make it a point to know as many people as you can in your industry and in related fields. Developing connections with people in other companies is extremely valuable in today's job market. The more people you know, the more potential opportunity you have.

Suppose you are a person who finds it difficult to blow your own horn persuasively. What do you do? Begin by building relationships based on mutual interests and make sure that your conversation includes your accomplishments. You don't need to brag or talk about your work until it bores others, but it is intelligent to let people know what you are doing and what you can do.

Marketing yourself is key when you are looking for a new position. When you have formed a habit of marketing yourself all of the time, you will not need to panic about this turning point. You will meet this challenge with an optimistic attitude, knowing that it is truly an opportunity.

You've already completed the hardest part. You've linked your background in an organized way to what you want to *do* and *be*. The challenge is to match your dreams, interests and expertise with the needs of your community. Keep in mind that your community is whatever you envision it to be - local, regional, national or global. Being valuable to the world is largely up to you. It is more important than ever to watch the future, to embrace the new impermanence and to stay sensitive to new demands for talents and skills so you can "do your thing" productively and with satisfaction.

Networking as second nature
Of course, most successful people do informal information interviews all the time. It can and should be done within one's current work life arrangement - with colleagues - as well as outside the current work situation, talking to peers, mentors, friends and family.

Effective networking requires mental clarity about your work life options based on your strengths and the work you enjoy. It helps greatly to possess or develop disciplined investigative and listening skills. Your primary objective is to learn what others think and feel about their jobs, their industry, long-term prospects, their work life environment, management, and competition. Your secondary or underlying objective is to obtain their assessment of how you might fit in with their current and future challenges and needs.

Here is more content for your Turning Points journal or online exercises. Use the journaling process to keep questions in your mind as you are networking. You can also use it to record what you learn from others. Gathering data about the world of work from your personal perspective and letting others be aware of who you are should be an ongoing activity. This process may be informal and relaxed if you are happily engaged at the present time, but intense and organized if you are in a voluntary or involuntary transition.

In addition to information interviewing, your initial market assessment should involve thorough research - keeping abreast of the world of work, whether it is your somewhat narrow field of interest or the larger world of constant change. You need to know what is happening and also what is likely to happen in the coming days, months and years. Choose your newspapers, professional journals and books with care. For the latest information from the U.S. Department of Labor on all kinds of career fields, find the Occupational Outlook Handbook website at http://www.bls.gov/oco/home.htm.

ALICIA

Alicia had been a secretary with a financial services firm before she became a full-time mom. When all the children were off to school, she volunteered to serve in a variety of financial roles with some community groups. These experiences exposed management issues involving her home town. She began to talk to civil servants and political activists about town governance and to educate herself on public policy issues regarding management and budgeting.

After a few more years, with the children out of the nest, she decided to run for political office, specifically for the local town government committee responsible for budgeting and taxation. Today, Alicia is the Chair of this committee.

Interviewing

A job interview is quite different from -and should *never* take place at the same time as - an information interview. Exploring the specific possibility of going to work for someone in a face-to-face meeting seems intimidating to most people. Fortunately, it usually is like performing: the butterflies disappear once you get on stage. That said, you *are* on stage, and rehearsals are essential.

Again, your journal or online exercises can come in handy. Write down details of the needs of the person, institution or organization that you can serve and the value you can contribute, based on prior conversations, articles or financial reports that may be available. Write down your specific job, career and life's work objectives. For each of the top five main characteristics you want the interviewer to recall about you, write down at least two examples of prior accomplishments which demonstrate what you can do. Remember, the two most powerful words you can say in an interview are, "For example..."

Based on a grading scale of Zero to Five (Five as high), good interviewers typically follow a checklist that looks something like this:

____ Candidate obtained valuable information from the interview
____ Candidate sought personal feedback
____ Candidate maintained a strong but not overbearing presence
____ Candidate answered questions clearly
____ Candidate listened well
____ Candidate communicated a positive attitude
____ Candidate communicated accomplishments well
____ Candidate's body language conveyed confidence and poise
____ Candidate maintained attention
____ Candidate's questions demonstrated an interest in developing an in-depth understanding of the position

Of course, you should have your own checklist. Interviewing is a two-way street. Even if you have formally applied for the job, you are still in the process of exploring how well it fits *your* criteria!

As with any other skill, interviewing is learned. You can improve with practice. Although it may feel awkward at first, ask your friends to interview you - especially if interviewing is part of their jobs. There are two specific skills you can practice that should help. First, tell stories. Rather than giving a basic, boring response to questions, use your examples to tell a good story with a beginning, middle, and end. Second, ask good questions. This will take the pressure off of you because your interviewer will be talking. It will also help you to evaluate the situation.

Keep an excellent and up-to-date resumé on hand
Everyone should have an up-to-date resume or a bio in their possession at all times. It facilitates recall and serves as a reminder to continuously market yours talents. It is much easier to document your accomplishments if you update them often rather than scrambling

to get your resume updated because you've just found your dream job and need to get your application submitted.

Technology certainly makes it easier to tailor resumes to each individual position to which you are applying. Because it is easy, it is also required. While it is necessary to keep an up-to-date resume on hand at all times, it is equally important to shape and adapt your resume to each specific job opportunity.

The art of the job description
Your resume is your marketing brochure, and your job descriptions are critical ways to "paint the picture" of your good works. A few simple rules will help your job descriptions to be compelling and vivid: 1) Use action verbs. Why use a passive verb when you can use an active and engaging action verb? 2) Use quantitative results and metrics wherever possible. Your employers want to know what your results were. The more you can use numbers, percentages and dollar figures in your job descriptions, the stronger they will be.

Typically, career counselors and executive search firms work with their clients to help them decide between a chronological or a functional format. In general, most hiring managers prefer chronological. All workers are going to have to become much more aware of their transferable skills as jobs and even entire businesses disappear over the years to come. We recommend using a hybrid of the Chronological and Functional resumes so that you can reap the benefit of both.

CHRONOLOGICAL RESUME
This traditional type of resume lists entries by category in reverse chronological order. Each experience is described in detail and highlights transferable skills, accomplishments, and responsibilities. This format is effective in conveying career continuity and professional growth.

FUNCTIONAL RESUME
The functional structure is more flexible and groups experiences by function or role rather than by date. For that reason, it can be especially useful when you are seeking a position in a new field or

you have an inconsistent work history. Unfortunately, the Functional Resume can be frustrating for the reader. Presenting yourself by function can leave people asking themselves "where?" or "when?" or even "for whom?"

HYBRID RESUME

The Hybrid Resume combines the best of both worlds. It is organized chronologically so it seems familiar to the reader. At the same time, it de-emphasizes gaps and highlights skills groups by categorizing by function. In other words, your job categories are functional (such as Teaching Experience, Management Experience, Accounting Experience, Training Experience) and yet within those categories the content is chronological.

Summary Points

- It is not enough to do a good job at work. You need to manage your career so you get credit for the good work you do.
- Make it a habit to document your successes and keep an accurate record of your accomplishments.
- Networking and conducting informational interviews both inside and outside your company are effective marketing strategies.
- Keep up the contacts.
- Keep an excellent and up-to-date resumé on hand.

Journal Subjects

- Make a list of ten or more people in your organization or industry whom you know well.
- Make a list of ten or more people in your company or industry whom you would like to know better.
- Make a list of primary targets for your personal public relations campaign.
- Develop a resume.

Chapter 13

FROM CRISIS TO OPPORTUNITY

"The turning point comes after a time of decay. Powerful light returns and a natural movement arises spontaneously. For that reason, the transformation of the old becomes easy with the old being discarded and the new introduced – both measure according with the time and therefore resulting in no harm and no mistakes are made."

-I Ching

For everything there is a time and a place. History is filled with stories of success and of failure separated only by a moment in time, a seemingly inconsequential choice, or by unexpected circumstances. One person was at exactly the right place in exactly the right time to take advantage of circumstances. Another took a vital step too late - or too soon. The key distinction was the timing of the turning point.

Living through crisis and turning it into opportunity is a very easy thing to talk about, and a very difficult thing to actually accomplish. Life is messy and no turning point will be without its ups and down. When you are immersed in the problem, your attitude is important. It can be very helpful to understand that *the crisis is the turning point.* At every moment, you have an opportunity to take a new path.

Have the Right Attitude

Being ready is important. Expect turning points. Be positive about your life and know there are inevitable changes ahead. Don't stick your head in the sand and think change won't happen. Denial never helps. By having the right attitude you will do a lot to make your future easier, healthier, happier and more successful. Begin your preparation for the future by establishing positive attitudes of expectation and exploration. Develop a sense of curiosity and adventure.

Learn something important from each Turning Point

Take advantage of the learning and insights each turning point can provide. Turn around and face the crisis head on. Look for the meaning and what you could possibly learn from the experience. While it is true that a turning point may seem terrible and depressing, it is important to remember that change is a healthy sign of an evolving, developing life. Many people fear change, and most of us find it difficult but, on the other hand, most of us also don't want to stay the same. Deep down we desire change. Major change may cause stress, but it is the only way to move in the direction of your dreams.

Negatives can be Positives

In a 2001 *Parade Magazine* article, Sylvester Stallone told his personal story of using negatives to accomplish positives.

SYLVESTER STALLONE

By his late twenties, Sylvester Stallone had become a $1.5 billion box office star. In the eyes of the public, the media, and his chosen industry, he was a complete success. Yet taking a long look at himself and his life – doing what he called a reality check - he didn't like what he saw. He was dating a different woman every month and living on film sets.

"I was in a whirlwind life," he said. "I didn't have the extraordinary love of my wife and children - I didn't have a real home. That started to get very, very old...I took a fierce emotional and moral inventory."

He thought about the failure of his two marriages, some serious problems his children were having and he began facing his regrets straight on.

"You never learn about yourself until you've been all the way down," he explained.

Stallone said, "When you've been pampered and protected and let other people think for you, you're going to eventually be at their mercy. When things start to go down, you can't expect them to rally. You have to do it for yourself. Maybe you'll win, maybe you won't. But if you don't fight back, you will never know what you're made of."

He started to see that his rapid rise to the top had blinded him to what is really important in life. "When you're living in the fast lane, you tend to overlook the basic components that give your life meaning: relationships, getting to know someone really well, putting someone else first. People who are highly ambitious often don't focus on the needs of their immediate family, especially their children."

Through the experience of digging into his own depths, Stallone developed new values for himself. He said, "I've been through the peaks and valleys. I understand now what is good for me. I can look at a goal and say I've climbed that mountain, and it's not worth the climb."

There will always be turning points you can't anticipate and certainly do not want. But you can make choices to use those negatives to create new positives. Life deals out *positive and negative* turning points. Some of these seem to be devastating and are really the impetus for needed change. They are the invitation we need to find a better way. Be ready to accept that invitation. Accept the fact that life can be difficult.

At the time of any turning point, it's important that you face three things squarely and with realism:

1. Yourself & Your Truth - the negatives in your nature as well as the positives. Ask yourself if you are an authentic person. Do you like yourself? If you cannot understand your own value and worth, you will never be able to convince others.

2. Your Situation – Understanding where you want to go requires that you know where you've been and where you are now. Have you attained the idealized

life you dreamed about? Is your career going the way you want? Is your job right for you? Is your home life the way you dreamed? Can you improve it or do you believe time will improve the situation if you are patient? You must take the time to assess your level or readiness for change and your willingness to take the necessary risks to obtain something greater.

3. Your Independence - No matter who you are, what your life is like, or who is in it, ultimately you are responsible for your own well-being. While we encourage you to strive for interdependence, connectedness and community, we also encourage you to avoid being overly dependent on anyone else.

This is the time to forge your real identity. Your new level of consciousness becomes clear. Through facing yourself, you can accurately evaluate and put things into place.

Take Steps to Lessen the Pain of a Crisis

Life breaks all of us, but some of us are stronger in the broken places.
                                                            -Ernest Hemingway

When you suffer severe stress from trying to deal with situations that are creating panic and confusion in your life, there are some things you can do to help yourself. Here are a few specific suggestions for handling those crisis situations which may come up in anyone's life.

GUIDELINES FOR CONVERTING CRISIS INTO OPPORTUNITY
Stand back and ask yourself these questions:

1. What is happening? What am I really looking at? Am I in denial?
2. How does this change the way I see my goals for the next period of my life?
3. Are there new obstacles now to reaching my goals?
4. Is there anything positive about this crisis?
5. Is my attitude helping or hurting?
6. What about my behavior?

7. Are there external circumstances I could change?
8. Are there some inner changes I could make?
9. What can I learn from this?
10. What's being asked of me?
11. Have I missed an earlier turning point?
12. Do I need to go back and complete the task I didn't finish then?
13. What resources are available (friends, family, counselors, etc) that can help me to navigate this transition?
14. How can I best take advantage of the changes that come with this turning point?

You may want to use these questions to look at some small issue in your life. It is a good idea to have the questions available for the next time a major turning point occurs. Remember that life is a series of turning points. Each crisis is also an opportunity for growth.

Best Wishes for Your Next Turning Point
We hope that this book has been helpful to you as you think about your next transition. You may be in the middle of a turning point, anticipating one, or trying to adjust to one. In our ever-changing world, we know that you will experience turning points again and again and we hope that you will come back to these pages if you've found them helpful.

Summary Points

- You can take definite steps to lessen the pain of a crisis.
- Continually question yourself.
- Have the right attitude.
- Learn something important from each turning point.
- Positives can emerge from negatives.

Journal Subjects

- Write a short summary of any events in your life that qualify as "devastating."
- Select one and write about how you handled the event, what you believed at the time it happened and how you see it now. Was there eventually a positive pay off?

Our Story

"Promise me you'll always remember. You're braver than you believe, stronger than you seem, and smarter than you think,"

-A.A. Milne

Turning Points was founded in the early 1980's by Phoebe and Jack Ballard. The Ballards had experienced Jack's retirement from a 35 year career in corporate America, and they were interested in assisting their friends and contemporaries in maximizing quality of life during their retirement years. The result of this effort was a series of training seminars and two books, the second of which was entitled: Turning Points: Create Your Path Through Uncertainty and Change.

In 2003, Jack and Phoebe's son, Mike, joined them in their quest to help bring these concepts to a broader audience. While developing a new online Turning Points tool, Mike met Dr. Lisa Severy, the newly appointed director of Career Services at the University of Colorado at Boulder. Sharing a passion for narrative career counseling and helping individuals maximize potential through thoughtful career transitioning, the Ballard-Severy collaboration developed naturally. Together Mike and Lisa taught a number of workshops for CU alumni in transition and, over time, the concept for a third book focusing specifically on career transitions emerged.

While writing, revising, and editing this new project, our new creative team experienced a monumental turning point of our own, the passing of Jack Ballard. Despite the enormous impact of his loss, we decided to continue with the book in Jack's honor. We believe he would be proud of the result and feel privileged that he was able to participate in its development.

Turning Points continues to grow and receive recognition for contributions to the field of career development. To find more about Turning Points, please go to www.TPNavigator.com.

INDEX

Printed in the United States
117558LV00003B/133-255/P